Violence and Mental Health in Everyday Life

Violence and Mental Health in Everyday Life

Prevention and Intervention Strategies for Children and Adolescents

Daniel J. Flannery

ALTAMIRA
PRESS

A Division of Rowman & Littlefield Publishers, Inc.
Lanham • New York • Toronto • Oxford

KH

To Caroline, who guides me and supports me every day, in every way. To Joseph, Patrick, Ellen, and Katie, who make being a parent so much fun. And to Jim and Judy, the best parents a kid could ever ask for.

ALTAMIRA PRESS
A division of Rowman & Littlefield Publishers, Inc.
A wholly owned subsidiary of The Rowman & Littlefield Publishing Group, Inc.
4501 Forbes Boulevard, Suite 200
Lanham, MD 20706
www.altamirapress.com

PO Box 317, Oxford, OX2 9RU, UK

British Library Cataloguing in Publication Information Available

Library of Congress Cataloguing-in-Publication Data

Flannery, Daniel J., 1962–
  Violence and mental health in everyday life : prevention and intervention strategies for children and adolescents / Daniel J. Flannery.
    p. ; cm. — (Violence prevention and policy series)
  Includes bibliographical references and index.
  ISBN 0-7591-0491-3 (cloth : alk. paper) — ISBN 0-7591-0492-1 (pbk. : alk. paper)
1. Children and violence—Psychological aspects. 2. Family violence—Psychological aspects. 3. Violence—Psychological aspects. 4. Violence in children. 5. Violence in adolescence. 6. Child mental health. 7. Teenagers—Mental health.
  [DNLM: 1. Mental Health—Adolescent. 2. Mental Health—Child. 3. Violence—prevention & control—Adolescent. 4. Violence—prevention & control—Child. 5. Violence—psychology—Adolescent. 6. Violence—psychology—Child. WS 350.8.A4 F585v 2005] I. Title. II. Series.
  RJ506.V56F55 2005
  618.92'8582—dc22

                                                      2005019010

Printed in the United States of America

⊗™ The paper used in this publication meets the minimum requirements of American National Standard for Information Sciences—Permanence of Paper for Printed Library Materials, ANSI/NISO Z39.48-1992.

9/19/06

CONTENTS

CONTENTS

TABLES AND FIGURES

Tables

Figures

ACKNOWLEDGMENTS

This volume would not have been possible without the support and encouragement of several friends and colleagues. I owe a special debt to Mark Fleisher, the series editor, who encouraged me to take on this project. I also thank Rosalie Robertson, Senior Editor at Alta-Mira Press who helped guide this effort from start to finish, and Jennifer Nemec for production support. Several anonymous reviewers provided excellent feedback. There are many colleagues whose work is reflected in these pages, and whose thoughts, reactions and comments I have come to trust over the years. Thanks to my wife and children, who allowed me to tell our stories. A special note of thanks to Mark Singer who has been a joy to work with and a special friend. To all my colleagues at the Institute, this volume would not have happened without their commitment and support for the work that we do every day, especially the dedication and wisdom of Dave Hussey and Mark Davis. And to all not noted here, whose work, thoughts, and stories fill the pages of this book, and who have influenced my thinking and my work over many years.

INTRODUCTION

I remember it well. I was sitting on the couch in our family room, and the television was blaring about terrorist threats and weapons of mass destruction in Iraq. Then the president came on for a live news conference. Katie, my then one-year-old daughter, was with me. She had just begun standing on her own and was perched between my legs, holding on to my hands, gently swaying back and forth. After the president finished speaking, I looked at Katie and said, "Well, honey, you're about to experience your first war." She looked at me, eyes wide open, as if to say, "Daddy, I don't understand!" Thinking back on that moment, I am both surprised and somewhat saddened by how casually I made the observation to her. I also remember feeling anxious about the world she was going to grow up in. What will she have to deal with when she gets older? Will she live in a world where violence is all around her, immediately available, part of her everyday life? If it is, how do I explain it to her? How do I make her feel safe? How do I make sure that she really is safe? How will she handle things when she's old enough to understand?

Katie is two and a half now, and the "conflict" in Iraq wages on, despite the president's declaration that the major fighting is over. While we have not recently experienced new terrorist acts in the United States, we are constantly reminded of soldier deaths, suicide bombings, terrorist networks, and military threats. It's a wonder that we're all not walking around as emotional wrecks, anxious and depressed, worried about what will happen next.

INTRODUCTION

Violence happens every day, in many different forms. It is not just a rare phenomenon that happens only to others, like being the victim of a homicide or stranger abduction. Violence takes place all around us: in our homes, in our relationships, in movies and television shows, in the computer and video games our children play, in our athletic games, and in the daily news. How we define violence will help determine how we deal with it. If we understand that violence occurs in many different ways in everyday life, then perhaps we will begin to understand its impact on our selves, on our children, on their development, and ultimately on our culture and our way of life. Dramatic, unpredictable violence certainly affects our mental health, especially when we are the direct victims of violence or when it happens to someone close to us. Violence significantly impacts an individual's mental health not just when it is dramatic or intense but also when it occurs in subtle ways every day. This includes the violence that we are exposed to every day in the media, as well as the incidents of aggressive behavior that occur daily on our roadways, in our shopping malls, and on the street. It includes violence related to domestic disputes and assault from siblings. This includes violence that children experience every day in our schools, from being exposed to incidents like threats and fighting to being bullied or victimized and harassed by peers. This is the unpredictable violence, or at least the threat of violence, occurring in our communities because of drugs and gangs, or because of terrorists whose only goal is to hurt as many unsuspecting people as possible.

Clearly many things influence violence and mental health at multiple levels. Individuals live in families and interact with peer groups and their own social networks. Families exist within neighborhoods that include schools, faith-based institutions, community centers, and various levels of support or, conversely, disorganization. For example, neighborhoods can vary in their level of gang activity, the availability of drugs, rates of mobility (families moving in and out of the neighborhood), levels of poverty, and the proportion of adults to children that live on a given street. Neighborhoods are embedded in larger communities and in systems such as the juvenile justice and law enforcement systems, the mental health systems, and the systems that serve children and families. Violence and mental health are affected by all of these layers and by how individuals, groups, levels, and systems interact with each other on a daily basis. My focus in this book is on individuals and families, with less emphasis on the structural, cultural, or political factors that influence violence and mental health, our reactions to violence, and our capacity to effectively cope with violence. These structural and contextual factors are discussed within each of the subsequent chapters as appropriate and as they relate to our overall understanding of violence and mental health.

In this book, I take a developmental perspective to try and help us understand violence, how it occurs in its many forms, and how it impacts mental health and our ability to cope on a daily basis. Rather than take a lifelong developmental view, this book focuses on development through adolescence. Infancy through adolescence is when the fundamental building blocks of lifelong development are formed. It is when we are first socialized to learn how to regulate our emotions and how to view and interpret the things going on around us in the world. It is when we are most likely to learn tolerance and respect for others, how to take control of our behavior, and to be responsible for our own successes and failures. It is when we learn language and the basic tools of problem solving and communication. It is the period of time when information-processing skills are formed and when our core social skills and competencies emerge. Infancy and childhood is when the bulk of brain development occurs, providing many of the ingredients that predict our risk for mental health problems later in life. It is when the genetics, hardware, and chemicals that influence our personalities, our temperament, and our ability to learn new things express themselves most clearly in development.

The goal of this book is to bring together current thinking and research in violence and mental health in a practicable way. In this book, I explore how young people experience violence in their everyday life and how this impacts their mental health and ability to cope with challenges and crises. This is not a textbook, but I try to bring to the reader what we know from the most current research about violence and mental health. Being informed is an important part of being able to cope effectively with things we can't always control or understand. This book does not address every possible aspect of violence, but it tries to provide some insight about how violence presents itself to young people, and it offers some suggestions about how to help them (and you) get through the day. At the end of the book, I offer information on a variety of professional resources, websites, and readings that are related to the topic of violence and mental health. If you don't find it here, maybe you'll find what you need there.

I hope this book is helpful to parents, teachers, social workers, child care workers, police officers, students, and others who interact every day with young people, to help them understand a little more about child development and how experiences with violence can affect development and daily life. What should we expect in different stages of development regarding the brain, socialization, learning, and mental health? Can a three-year-old be depressed? Can an infant, who is not yet able to speak or process information, really be affected by chronic exposure to domestic violence? Are some children predisposed to become violent? Why do some children appear to be so very resilient when faced with adversity, while others seem to have everything crumble at the first sign of stress or problems in their lives? How many kids and families are affected by serious mental health issues? And, finally, what do we do about all of this? How do we help kids exposed to violence cope effectively with what is going on in the world around them? How do we prevent things from getting worse? What are the clues that we can pick up on when a child is young that will let us know the child may struggle with sustaining mental health? Is there evidence that early identification and prevention actually help?

I attempt to address these and many other questions in this volume. I draw as much from personal experience as I do from current research in violence and mental health, but always with an eye toward making the concepts practical and understandable for everyday life. What does my personal experience have to do with this? First of all, I grew up in a large family (the second oldest of eight), and I have four children of my own who have provided me the fodder for many of the stories and examples I write about in this book. Joseph, our oldest, is ten and in the fifth grade. At age five, he was diagnosed with type 1 diabetes and has been insulin dependent ever since. Patrick is eight, in the third grade, and the natural athlete of the family. Ellen is six and in the first grade. She still loves to play school when she is done with her homework at night. Katie, our youngest, is almost two, right in the middle of learning to talk in sentences and use the potty. My wife, Caroline, is a special education teacher, which luckily gives her the experience and patience to cope with her spouse and the many challenges our children bring to our days.

Professionally, I have been a licensed and practicing clinical psychologist for the past fifteen years, and most of my work has been with children, adolescents, and families. For the past five years, I have been a professor at a university, leading a research institute that focuses on violence prevention from many different perspectives. The institute conducts work in the areas of mental health, schools, law enforcement, public health, and substance abuse. Some of what you will read about involves the research we are doing at the institute, as well as the work being done by my colleagues in violence and mental health around the world. Much of my work over the years has involved the provision of training and workshops on violence and mental health to groups including parents, teachers, law enforcement and probation officers, and public health workers like doctors and nurses. I draw on the topics I've presented in these trainings and on the most frequently asked questions to guide what I cover in this volume.

This book is loosely organized around development. I begin with a brief discussion of how we define violence and mental health and what it means to cope effectively on a day-to-day basis. This is followed by a thorough discussion of brain development and how it is related to violence (both the risk for being aggressive or violent and how violence impacts development of the neurochemistry of the brain). Several chapters are then devoted to violence and mental health from a developmental perspective, from family violence and violence in childhood and adolescence to violence at schools and how youth are affected by violence in the media. The book ends with chapters specifically devoted to coping strategies, to investigating the link between violence and mental health, and to recommendations for prevention, intervention, and policy.

Within each chapter, I discuss issues of gender, culture, or economic status (e.g., poverty) whenever appropriate. With respect to gender, for example, research tells us how boys and girls differ in their exposure to violence, their rates of victimization, and how likely they are to act violently against others. Boys and girls are also socialized differently regarding how they deal with stressors and pressures and how they approach and solve problems. They differ in the timing and types of mental health symptoms they experience (e.g., depression, anger, anxiety) and in how they express themselves in their behavior toward others. Girls are more likely to internalize their feelings and experience symptoms such as depression and anxiety, for example, whereas boys are more likely to act out their behavior toward others and be more angry and aggressive. This is not always the case, and we'll discuss instances where girls appear to display more mal-adaptive aggression and anger than even the most violent males. One rule of development should always be kept in mind: there are always exceptions to the rules.

CHAPTER ONE
VIOLENCE AND MENTAL HEALTH: IS ANYTHING NORMAL ANYMORE?

If we want to understand violence, we need to start with figuring out what it is. Violence takes on many forms and occurs in many different settings and contexts. It is a complex behavior, one that is not easily explained or predicted. If we were so good at predicting who would become violent, we would do a better job of picking out school shooters, individuals who randomly shoot at motorists at gas stations and on highways, and those who kill their coworkers over some workplace dispute. We would be able to identify them long before the violent act occurred. As it is, we have yet to develop any foolproof way of picking out who will act violently toward others and when, and under what circumstances violence will occur. We know that the likelihood of a person's being violent increases when certain risk factors are present, and decreases when an individual possesses certain social skills and personality characteristics or grows up with certain support systems and opportunities in place. Of course, not every person who is at risk becomes violent, and not every person who enjoys lots of positive support avoids acting in an aggressive, violent manner at some point in time over the life course.

The first step toward understanding violence and its impact on mental health is to be able to accurately describe what it is and how an individual comes to act in an aggressive, violent way toward others. Most of us are exposed to violence in one form or another on a fairly regular basis. Being exposed to violence means you can either be witness to violent behavior or be victimized by violence. Both increase one's risk in the future of acting violently against someone else. Perpetrating violence can range from being aggressive to engaging in behavior like fighting or bullying, to inflicting injury upon someone else (with or without a weapon), to killing someone else (homicide). When we refer to perpetrating violence in this book, we are generally referring to violence between two people, sometimes called interpersonal violence. We will not be discussing (at least not at any great length) the act of self-injury or suicide, sometimes referred to as intrapersonal violence. Further, in this book I am focusing mostly on violent behavior that is intentional and purposeful rather than accidental. When someone is accidentally hurt (e.g., your child fell off his bike or out of a tree), this is referred to as unintentional injury.

I define mental health in everyday life a lot like coping: how well is someone able to adapt to crises and stressors and function in everyday life? In this book, I am not focusing on severe forms of mental illness like bipolar disorder or schizophrenia, although the issue of mental health and mental disorders is addressed in the chapter on the relationship between violence and mental health. Rather, I focus in this book on the less severe manifestations of mental health problems (relatively speaking) like depression and mood disorders, anxiety, anger and impulse control, and post-traumatic stress disorder (PTSD) symptoms. There are sometimes serious symptoms and consequences associated with these mental health problems, like an inability to socialize, difficulties at school, and problems with getting along with others. Many individuals who experience significant mental health problems find benefit from counseling, therapy, or the use of medications. However, for most individuals, these mental health symptoms are not serious enough to be completely or permanently debilitating or to require long-term hospitalization. If mental health symptoms impact an individual's ability to cope on a daily basis, however, they become important for that person and others around them. The main premise of this book is that violence affects everyone in some form, and our daily experiences with violence via exposure, victimization, or perpetration significantly affect our mental health and ability to cope. Sometimes these difficulties are transient, expectable consequences of experiencing something sudden or traumatic, but there are also longer-term consequences for our mental health from chronic, pervasive exposure to violence.

Victimization from Violence

In the United States alone, it is estimated that at least 5 million children are victims of violence or are witnesses to physical abuse, domestic violence, or violence in their neighborhoods and communities. In addition to being exposed to violence, an individual can be a victim of violence. According to one study that combined data from a series of national surveys, child victimization ranges from being the victim of extraordinarily rare acts of violence, such as homicide and stranger abduction, to being a victim of ongoing physical or sexual abuse or of a random act of violence. Being a homicide victim is the rarest event for children, occurring at a rate of .03 per 1,000 youth in the United States. Further along the continuum, 23 of every 1,000 children report that they are victims of physical abuse. More common forms of victimization include being harassed by a bully, being verbally threatened, or being the victim of a theft. Victimization from theft is reported by nearly half of all children under the age of eighteen, 497 of every 1,000 youth. The most common type of victimization from violence, reported by 800 of every 1,000 children under age eighteen in the United States, is assault from a sibling.[1] Over half of the 800 youth also report that assaults from siblings are serious enough that they resulted in an injury requiring medical treatment, like a trip to the emergency room or a visit to a doctor's office. Rates of sibling assault are nearly double the next most frequent form of victimization reported by children, being the victim of physical punishment (e.g., getting into a fight), which occurs at a rate of 499 per 1,000 youth.

This continuum of violence victimization among children raises the question of what is "normal" or "expectable" regarding aggressive or violent behavior, and of what should concern us with respect to the impact of victimization on a child's mental health, resilience, and coping. Isn't fighting among siblings a common occurrence? Weren't many of us victimized by an older sibling (more than once), and didn't we come out OK? We suffer no serious emotional scars, right? I came from a large family of four boys and four girls. I am number two in the pecking order, second only to my brother, eleven months my senior. This meant that the two of us had plenty of opportunities to victimize our younger siblings, and we took every advantage of them. We were either trying to get them into trouble, getting back at them for getting us into trouble, or just being nasty to get what we wanted. Sibling assault (or fighting between brothers and sisters) takes on many forms and is a common occurrence in most homes, particularly when there are many children who live in a single home. It can include siblings slapping each other for no apparent reason as they walk by each other or fighting over ownership of toys, clothes, or food. Sibling assault can even be said to occur when an older sibling forces a younger sibling to do his chores. Because fighting (and subsequent injury) among siblings is so common, should we just expect it to happen and accept it as normal?

I don't think we should be so fast to judge on this one. Victimization in any form, even if it occurs from common and "expectable" events like fighting between siblings, should be taken as a serious threat to a child's mental health and functioning. Let's say you are walking down an alley one evening after a nice dinner at a local restaurant. You are approached by a stranger who quickly sidles up beside you, points a gun at you, and demands that you give him your wallet. Startled, you quickly oblige while blurting out something unintelligible. The stranger does not hurt you, and you do not know who he is. You will most likely never see him again. You have just been victimized by an act of violence (or at least an act of serious aggression). It is hopefully not something that occurs to you on a regular basis, so this is a relatively rare event. And yet, after this occurs, you cannot help feeling vulnerable, feeling angry, feeling violated, feeling extremely wary and anxious the next time you are walking down the street alone or in a dark alley. You'll probably avoid going to that restaurant again for a long while to avoid the feelings you associate with the memory of being robbed.

Let's briefly compare the two events and then decide which has more of an impact on an individual's mental health and well-being. Assault from a sibling may be a relatively common event in your household. Being the victim of a robbery is a relatively rare event. Your sibling sometimes injures you in a fight or with an object or weapon (a rubber band or pair of scissors, for example) so that you need medical treatment. The person who took your wallet did point a gun at you but did not physically hurt you. Your sibling (or parent for that matter) is someone known to you, someone that you love (and who presumably cares for you), and someone that you see every day. The stranger who robbed you is none of those things. Your home is where you live as a child. You did not choose your home, nor did you choose your siblings. You have little choice about staying or leaving; at least you have few options about where else you could go. So, you just live there and take the abuse or the beatings from your sibling as best you can. As an adult, you can avoid that alley again, stay away from the restaurant, stop carrying cash, or arm yourself to defend against another random assault. As a robbery victim, most people would assert that the incident was significantly upsetting to them, that it may have permanently altered their sense of safety and well-being, and that it may even have contributed to feelings of post-traumatic stress like depression, anxiety, and fearfulness. How can we so quickly dismiss the sibling assault, especially if the assault occurs on a regular basis? Isn't it likely to have the same effect on a young child, maybe even more of an effect if it occurs repeatedly over time? This kind of victimization can significantly affect child well-being and mental health. We can't ignore the possibility. We can't dismiss the potential negative impact of events on child mental health and coping just because those events seem to be a "normal" or "expectable" part of daily life. Sometimes daily life is nasty and negative, and the things that occur as part of our day, like violence, have a significant impact on our mental health and well-being.

What Does It Mean to Be Mentally Healthy?

When discussing the impact of violence on mental health in everyday life, I am focusing on mental health with respect to being able to cope effectively with the stressors and challenges of daily life, including the unexpected and sometimes seriously violent incidents that we are exposed to either directly via victimization or indirectly via the media or other mechanism (e.g., hearing gunshots in your neighborhood). Being mentally healthy does not mean that one never experiences a sense of anxiety or never feels depressed. Anxiety and fear are normal and expectable reactions to serious incidents or threats to our safety and security. Sometimes people have a good reason why they are feeling depressed. If a child's dog gets hit by a car, she will feel sad and depressed for several days or more. If grandparents become ill or pass away, you expect children to be sad or to not feel like going to school for a while. Children may also have lots of questions about adults leaving them or be worried that other adults in

11

their life will also die. These are normal, expectable responses to events in one's life. The problem occurs if the depressed mood persists, if the anxiety becomes so pervasive that it begins to impact one's daily life and functioning. This is when one should consider seeking additional help via medical evaluation or therapy. If a child is so depressed that he stops eating or stays in bed all day or begins speaking about hurting himself, then this goes beyond the normal ups and downs of moodiness. If a child is depressed without knowing why or without your being able to identify a reason for her sadness, then maybe there is some chemical or physical basis for her mood that should be explored and that may need professional assessment or treatment.

From Aggression to Violence

As I discuss different forms of violence and violent behavior, I will be discussing what we know about aggression, bullying, delinquency, conduct disorder, and violence. It is important to understand how these terms are different and how they overlap, because while we often use them interchangeably, they do represent different constellations of behavior, developmentally and with respect to intensity and seriousness of the behavior. At the lower end of the continuum of behavior, aggression is the term most often used to describe behavior of young children and milder forms of violent behavior. This includes behaviors like fighting, kicking, spitting, and cutting in line. It might also refer to nonphysical behavior like threats, harassment, and intimidation. Aggression is also studied as a personality trait. Some people appear to be more aggressive than others, meaning that their daily functioning is more likely to be characterized by these types of behavior than is the daily functioning of someone who is temperamentally more passive or soft-spoken. Lastly, aggression and aggressive behaviors seem to be the baseline or starting point from which the other, more serious behaviors develop or emerge later in life.

Bullying is most often discussed with respect to school-age youth who are perpetrating violence and aggression against others (this is discussed in more detail in the chapter on school violence). Bullying is typically characterized by threats, intimidation, and physical fighting. The perpetrator is usually bigger than the victim and may be older, although bullying of a same-age peer is also common.

Delinquency is a formal term used in the juvenile justice system to describe youth who engage in offenses like truancy, running away, minor theft, substance use, vandalism, fighting, or incorrigibility. In juvenile justice terms, a youth can be "adjudicated delinquent," which means that he has engaged in some form of behavior inappropriate for a child under the age of eighteen (or sixteen in some states), and there can be formal consequences imposed on the youth (or his parents) as a result of the delinquent behavior.

Conduct disorder is the psychological term used when formally diagnosing a child with a psychiatric disorder characterized by inappropriate levels of aggressive or violent behavior. Conduct disorder is characterized by more serious and persistently aggressive or violent behavior that is directed toward others (e.g., fighting or assaults that result in serious injury) or that involves the physical destruction of property (e.g., vandalism, fire setting). A child can develop conduct disorder symptoms very early on, prior to the age of ten or later, with onset during the adolescent years. The developmental prognosis is worse for a child whose conduct problems begin at a younger age, when the problems are characterized by more serious forms of aggressive or violent behavior, and when the problems co-occur with other difficulties like substance use, school failure, or attention-deficit/hyperactivity disorder (ADHD).

Antisocial behavior is another psychiatric term used to describe adolescents and adults who continue to engage in serious conduct-disordered behavior persistently over time and who thus have developed an antisocial personality disorder. For example, while a large majority of youth who engage in delinquent or conduct-disordered behavior in adolescence will no longer do so in young adulthood (they essentially "age out" of criminal behavior), a percentage of youth will continue to do so well into adulthood, and may even escalate the frequency and intensity of their aggressive, violent behavior. For instance, there exists a high percentage of adult felony offenders in our correctional system who would meet the formal diagnostic criteria for an antisocial personality disorder.

Violent behavior is usually reserved for the most serious forms of aggressive behavior, and for behavior that is perpetrated against other persons (e.g. interpersonal assault). There is a developmental context for violence, however, in that it is highly unusual for a five-year-old to perpetrate homicide against another person or to sexually assault someone else.

So, when we assess violent behavior among five-year-olds, we are not typically asking them if they carry weapons or if they are sexually active. These behaviors are much more characteristic developmentally of adolescents and adults. Among young children, we have assessed behaviors such as threats to harm another person, physical fighting that results in injury, hitting someone else first before being hit, and attacking someone else with a weapon like a knife or a gun. These behaviors are considered to be much more serious than aggressive behaviors like fighting without a weapon, cutting in line, or calling someone else a name.

Are these rare behaviors that only occur in unusual circumstances among young people? Unfortunately, the answer is no. If fact, these aggressive and violent behaviors occur more frequently among young children than you might expect. Table 1.1 reflects the percentage of boys and girls in both elementary and high school who admitted to engaging in different types of aggressive or violent behavior at least once in the past year.[2] Generally, rates of engaging in aggressive or violent behavior are higher for boys than they are for girls, a trend that has been illustrated over and over again in research on violence (although rates among females are rising faster than rates among males). Further, while rates of violent behavior generally increase with age, there are some notable exceptions, particularly for the Ohio sample that includes middle school students (grades three through eight), which is different from the Arizona sample (grades three through six) and the Ohio-Colorado high school sample (grades nine through twelve). Both girls and boys in the middle school sample reported higher rates of threatening someone, hitting someone after being hit, and beating someone up (over 20 percent higher) than high school students did. The rates for beating someone up are much higher in the elementary school sample than in the high school sample.

Do all kids act this way? While no study is perfect or can claim to absolutely reflect how any one child will act in all situations, these data represent information gathered from over 12,000 students from three states in three separate studies conducted over a ten-year period. The samples are also geographically and ethnically diverse and include students from urban, suburban, and rural schools, as well as students from diverse family situations and socioeconomic statuses. The bottom line is that these data are not unusual but pretty typical of the types of aggressive, violent behavior that young people admit to engaging in.

Table 1.1. Violent Behavior Among Children and Adolescents*

ACT	Arizona Elementary		Ohio Elem./ Middle		Ohio/Colorado High School	
	Boys	Girls	Boys	Girls	Boys	Girls
Threatened someone	36.4	25.1	53.5	40.9	57.6	37.1
Hit someone before being hit	47.3	35.0	54.3	44.5	57.9	47.4
Hit someone after being hit	66.7	56.5	82.2	71.5	74.6	66.7
Beaten someone	51.8	29.3	56.3	38.0	32.2	16.3
Attacked someone with a knife	9.6	3.5	5.3	4.8	8.6	5.9
Shot at someone	N/A	N/A	N/A	N/A	18.4	3.3

* Percentage Admitting to the Behavior Within the Past Year

Each of the different ways we define and describe aggressive and violent behavior conveys some important information about the seriousness of the behavior being assessed, about what is appropriate or inappropriate given the age or developmental status of the person engaging in that behavior, and about the long-term risk that the individual will eventually engage in serious delinquent behavior, become involved in a gang, develop a serious conduct disorder or antisocial personality disorder, or become incarcerated. Of course, there exist many other problems that can compound an individual's risk of becoming violent. We will examine some of the different types of violent behavior later when we address the question of how children grow up to become violent.

Normal Development Gone Awry: Hidden Psychopathology

We're all affected by the hidden psychopathology of everyday life. How often have you been surprised to find out that the person you thought was normal, stable, and all together happened to be struggling with some significant personal, family, financial, or legal issue? We all have them, the skeletons in our past, the family issues that everyone would be surprised to hear about, or the financial stressors that sometimes lead us to feel desperate and hopeless or to do stupid things. Sometimes the hidden psychopathology has to do with our mental health, which is certainly affected by all of the other stressors and hardships that seem to pop up on a regular basis. This is one of the vagaries of coming from a large family: in many ways it represents the best of times, and at others, the worst of times. There are more siblings, cousins, and relatives to enjoy the holidays with, to depend on for support, and to share your struggles with as you try to figure out how to raise your children and provide for your family. But strength in numbers also brings with it added opportunity to experience pain, hardship, loss, and suffering. Just by sheer numbers alone, you are bound to be exposed to more troubles, more crises, and more challenges that emerge every day.

The number of people struggling with significant mental health issues in this country is staggering, and they aren't showing any signs of declining. The number of people on antidepressants is at an all-time high. We have diagnosed (and medicated) more children with ADHD than anyone knew even existed. Great debate continues about whether we are medicating children who do not need it, or whether we are using medication as a way to control unruly child behavior. Rates of autism, schizophrenia, and bipolar disorder (what used to be called manic depression) are all on the rise. There exists some validity to the claim that rates rise as we become more aware of a problem and therefore get better at reporting it. This is true in studies of parent-adolescent conflict, for example. As soon as you begin to help parents understand how to utilize appropriate strategies to discipline and communicate with their children, reported rates of conflict and relationship problems increase because parents are identifying certain behaviors as problems, whereas before they just thought things were part of the normal way parents and adolescents behaved.

This is partly the struggle of trying to understand and figure out what constitutes "normal." For example, I'm not sure there exists a "normal" family structure anymore. Families are composed of a variety of different people, some biologically related, some related by association or time, some by extension, and some by necessity. When we talk about family relationships today, we may be referring to two parents and their biological children, but this family structure is quickly creeping into the minority. We're just as likely to be talking about a single parent (no longer just mom raising the kids), and increasingly so grandparents raising their grandchildren. We have more women having children late in life without a married partner, and more nontraditional couples adopting children.

One way to define normal is to assess a behavior relative to what is most common. This is a problem, however, when the most common or acceptable behavior is deviant or problematic. If a society deems intolerance of an ethnic group acceptable or ostracizes members of a religious faith, does this make the intolerance normal just because it is common or acceptable (or expectable?). It seems to me that "normal" also implies "well-adjusted" by some common, universal criteria. Normal implies a lack of deviance, not just being average or typical. Normal development follows a particular sequence and structure, for example. The fetus will mature normally if development occurs in a specific sequence—torso and internal organs before outer limbs, fingers, and toes. The head develops before the trunk, the brain stem before the outer layers of the brain. If any of these things occurs out of order, bad things happen. Children develop certain cognitive skills, language, and motor skills over time in an expectable sequence of increasing complexity and organization. Concrete thinking comes before abstract thought, balance comes before running, and babbling precedes speaking in complete sentences. When there are delays in reaching certain developmental milestones, when something is missing in the sequence, or when something occurs out of order, then we begin to suspect that problems may emerge in normal development, which has somehow gone awry.

The same concepts can apply to mental health and development. Sometimes normal development goes awry and problems develop. These problems can lead to significant challenges in maintaining our mental health on an everyday basis. The bottom line is that everybody has something that they deal with every day. Just scratch the surface. We are anxious, or we're depressed, or we think about being too tired and hopeless to even get out of bed in the morning. We have obsessive thoughts about being safe or being clean or whether we shut off the iron and locked the doors before leaving the house. We worry about our siblings, about our aging parents, and about whether our nieces and nephews are doing well in school. We worry about when we'll get that next phone call in the middle of the night telling us that something horrible has happened. We worry about whether our children fit in and whether they are making friends at school. We worry about the future and whether our kids will be able to go to college and get a good job when they reach adulthood. We worry about money, about our health care, about our access to things we need, and about having the opportunity to be successful. We want to keep up with the Joneses and have enough stuff and toys to make us happy. We want to see the world but worry that the world is less and less safe and more and more unpredictable (like what's been going on in Spain and London on commuter trains). We worry about the world that our children are growing up in and about what will be in store for them as they grow old. We worry about what will happen to them when we aren't around anymore to carry their backpacks or make their lunches or tell them to clean up their rooms and to take a shower (this week, at least). We want the best for them, and the best for us, and we put on a brave face and make it through each day, hoping and expecting that the next day will be better. We hope that we will be able to cope with whatever comes along—good, bad, or indifferent.

The good news (amidst all the worry) is that things are getting better, at least in some respects. While we all have more to deal with (more daily stressors, more financial strain, more family issues), there are also many more resources out there to help us get through the problem times. These resources, especially information about things, are also more immediately available via the Internet. Remember when the only option for finding out about the mysterious rash you had was to ask a neighbor to look at it or for Dad to pull out the family health medical book and guess? That was hit-or-miss medicine at its best, and I'm living proof that Spam and chicken soup were not cure-alls for every ailment that wasn't identified in the book. Technology and treatments for illnesses have advanced rapidly in the last two decades, so things that used to make us very ill or would threaten our very life are now more manageable and treatable. People are more aware of what goes on in the world around them. There are fewer surprises. There may be more things that are unpredictable or unstable, but this is different from being completely unexpected. Unpredictability can create a different kind of problem, but knowledge gains are faster and are utilized more efficiently today than ever before because we are more aware and because things are more available to us than they ever were. Despite the many challenges I talk about in this book, I do it with a clear sense of hopefulness that things will continue to get better, at least for our children and grandchildren, if not for me and you.

What's the DIF?

How do we decide if a behavior is a problem or whether it has gone beyond what we expect and would consider normal? Let's take an example.

A mom calls me up, the clinical psychologist, and says to me over the phone, "My son is getting into fights and wetting the bed at night! What do I do?" What is the first question I ask that mom?

The first question I ask her is, "What kind of insurance do you have?" (I wish I was kidding). This has, unfortunately, become a necessity of our mental health system of care (and perhaps the focus of a whole other book). The next question I ask her, before anything else, should be, "How old is your child?" The first step in understanding whether a particular behavior is a problem is to place it in developmental context. What is a problem for a ten-year-old may not be a problem for a four-year-old. Let's go back to the problem. Bed wetting may be fairly normal for a four-year-old but somewhat problematic for a ten-year-old, depending on a number of features regarding the target behavior. The same goes for fighting.

How do we make a relatively quick decision about whether the stated problem is of great concern or is more normal? One rubric that I've used, and that I sometimes teach to law enforcement professionals and teachers, is to ask yourself the question, with respect to the behavior of interest, "What's the DIF?" Table 1.2 illustrates what each letter of the acronym stands for.

When considering together the duration, intensity, and frequency of any behavior, one can make a relatively quick determination about whether the behavior is a significant problem that may require further assessment or intervention. Placing the behavior in a developmental context can also help you determine if the behavior is normal or expectable for that child's age, or whether a more serious problem exists.

The same rubric can be used to assess the appropriateness of a child's aggressive behavior. Is ripping a toy away from another child for no reason

Table 1.2. Assessing Behavior

D	Duration	When did the behavior start? How long has it been going on? Was there some event that triggered the bed wetting? Is the onset recent or is this a long-term problem?
I	Intensity	How bad is it when the behavior occurs? Do fights always lead to injury and the need for medical treatment, or are arguments more likely to be verbal spats, more bothersome and oppositional than assaultive and violent?
F	Frequency	How often does this happen? Does your child get into fights every day or once a month? Does he wet the bed every night or only when he sleeps in the basement on weekend?

a problem? It may be for your six-year-old, but it is relatively normal for a two-year-old. Does that mean when it happens with your two-year-old you pat her on the head and, smiling, say, "Good girl!" No, but should you be worried that your two-year-old will grow up to be a bully? Not necessarily. If the behavior persists over time and your child begins to act aggressively with other children and adults, at home and at day care, with siblings and with strangers, would you have more reason to be concerned? Yes, but still there may be some reason for the way your child behaves, and again it does not mean your child will grow up to become an antisocial, rejected bully incapable of getting along well with others.

Finding the Source of the Problem

We had a similar dilemma not too long ago with our eight-year-old son Patrick. When he was five, and continuing for a time as a six-year-old, Patrick would sometimes become extremely frustrated and annoyed with things. When Patrick got angry about something, he would act out impulsively and aggressively toward objects in his path, such as furniture. He might, for example, shove aside a chair as he walked past. We weren't really sure what was going on. Did this happen when he was tired? Was he frustrated when he didn't get his way? Did he get angry when we asked him to do something he didn't feel like doing? Was it worse when we interrupted something (like when he was lying on the couch and watching TV)? At first it seemed worse right after school, when he was transitioning from the school day back to home. It felt like it was a little bit of all of the above, and we were worried. My wife and I talked about whether he needed help beyond what we could do for him at home as Mom and Dad. If we tried to sit down and speak with him about it, he turned us off or dismissed us with a quick, loud "OK!" which really didn't mean "OK." It really meant, "leave me alone."

Patrick, you should know, is a fierce competitor on the athletic field and takes his schoolwork very seriously. He is used to getting mostly As on his report card. To his credit, Patrick's conduct and effort are always noted by his teachers to be exemplary. He likes his stuff to be neat. His desk at school is pristine, and his printing looks like it comes off a computer. So, for all the frustrations and problems with anger we were having at home, this was clearly not going on at school, and our discussions with the parents of his friends told us that he was not acting out when over at someone else's house to play. We were confused and worried. What were we doing wrong?

One day we got a progress report from school. Patrick was struggling with reading—struggling hard. They wanted him to go see a tutor. They wanted him to "go out to the silver trailer," as he put it, "where the kids who can't do their schoolwork go." His teacher said Patrick had all the pieces and parts but wasn't putting them together very well. He was not keeping up with the rest of the class. What were we to do?

Joseph, our oldest, kicked it into high gear. He immediately offered to help Patrick learn to read, especially after witnessing our struggles sitting down with Patrick at night and him flinging his body around the couch as he became more and more frustrated with not doing it well. Joe set up his own token economy in their bedroom, gathering lots of miscellaneous toys, Pokémon cards, and school supplies, and then labeling each with a number of points Patrick could earn for reading a certain amount of time with him each night. My wife and I thought, "Now, how awesome is that?"

The token system worked for a little while, maybe a couple of weeks, but Patrick still struggled and was still getting frustrated. It was clear he needed more help. We sat down with him and talked about going to the trailer. Pat would have nothing to do with it. He simply refused. We were so concerned that he needed help with his reading that we decided to send him to a private tutoring service where one of his teachers worked part-time. The results were fantastic, and Patrick is now, a year later, caught up with his peers and is no longer frustrated every day with reading. His tantrums are gone, his sense of humor and easygoing personality are back, and he is doing well in all of his school subjects, reading included (although he gets a B in reading and an A in almost everything else, he still points this out when he gets his report card).

What's the point of the story? We thought long and hard about whether Patrick needed some extra help to manage his anger and frustration. We talked to his teachers, who insisted that he was not a behavior problem in the classroom. We talked about how often it occurred and how bad it was when he acted out. Patrick never physically attacked any of his siblings or his parents, but if out of anger he had, I think we would have gotten him some other kind of help right away. How long had this been going on? We could pretty much trace it back to when reading became more of a daily homework task, when reading groups were being formed at school, and when kids were naturally comparing themselves on how much they were reading each week. How often was it happening? Not very often, although when it did, we were concerned with his seeming inability to control his frustration. Developmentally, was this normal? Five-year-olds often have trouble controlling their emotions (self-regulating) and expressing their anger and frustration in appropriate ways. In the end, my wife and I decided that, while Patrick was definitely having trouble and we should pay attention to it, his troubles were not so unusual or unique that he needed immediate extra intervention or assessment for behavior or mental health issues. We were fortunate that we were able to identify something that seemed to be causing a lot of his anger and frustration and was contributing to his lack of self-confidence and hopelessness about the situation. Patrick's reading problem made him more anxious and irritable, which further increased the likelihood that he would act out when frustrated.

It is not always easy to decide whether something is normal and expectable or whether it deserves more serious attention or professional help. People (especially children) are unpredictable and inconsistent (the most consistent thing about our kids, sometimes, is that they are inconsistent). Circumstances and situations change, affecting our judgment and ability to compare behavior and reactions to things over time. A general rule of thumb to follow is that if the problem or stressor begins to affect how an individual functions on a daily basis, or if there occurs a noticeable change in behavior, mood, or relationships, a more serious look and greater attention is warranted. The longer the problem or change persists, the more likely it is that significant action or intervention is necessary. Never be afraid to seek out help when you need it. None of us has all the answers, and sometimes being Mom or Dad is more important to our kids than being therapist, teacher, doctor, or spiritual advisor. Sometimes we need to hear it from somebody else before we (or our kids) will believe it. This works with basketball, hockey, and gymnastics, so maybe it will work with our kid's behavior, school performance, and mental health as well.

Start from the Beginning

To understand behavior and mental health, we first need to understand the brain and how it develops, because ongoing research shows us that the structure, function, and chemicals in our brain significantly influence development, behavior, and health. Let's turn now to looking at the brain and how it develops in children and adolescents.

HOW DOES THE BRAIN DEVELOP? SETTING THE STAGE FOR LATER MENTAL HEALTH

How and when the brain develops is crucial to determining child outcomes such as social and emotional competence, achievement, and resilience. Historically, we used to think that almost all of the important facets of brain development occurred in utero and during the first three to five years of life. While much occurs during this initial period of development, we have recently begun to learn, through the use of new technology such as brain mapping, that additional developments in the brain occur between the ages of four and twelve, and that some critical brain growth and pruning even occurs into late adolescence and young adulthood.[1]

The potential effectiveness of early prevention or intervention is highlighted by what we know about brain development. During the early years, a child's brain is capable of reorganizing itself in response to environmental influences, particularly during crucial learning periods when connections between brain cells are being made and broken down at an enormous rate. Critical windows of development occur in phases between birth and about age twelve, during which the foundations for thinking, language, attitudes, overall ability, and coping strategies are laid.[2] Once the windows close, much of the basic and fundamental architecture of the brain is completed and becomes very difficult to change or reverse. In practical terms, this means that the learning of new skills, capacities, and competencies becomes much more difficult after age twelve.[3]

Environment and the Brain

In general, the brain develops in the following way.[4] During fetal development, brain cells are created and assigned general jobs. After birth, a second wave of structural change occurs as an enormous number of connections, called synapses, are made between brain cells. Between birth and about eight months of age, for example, the number of connections grows from about 50 trillion to 1,000 trillion. Connections are essentially overproduced so that the brain is capable of adapting to a host of different environmental stimuli and sensory experiences. The experiences that are reinforced or repeated often form firm connections in the brain, sort of like integrated maps that contribute to the brain's long-term infrastructure. Connections that are not reinforced are pruned away (i.e., they die off) because they are not used or because the brain decides they are not needed. The number of synaptic connections peaks at about eight months of age, but significant connections continue to be made through age three. From this peak, a critical restructuring of the brain occurs between the ages of four and twelve, determined by what is used and what is not used on a day-to-day basis.

The are also several core principles of neurodevelopment that must be considered when understanding how environmental experiences affect the brain: (1) both genes and environment influence brain development; (2) the brain develops in a sequential and hierarchical fashion; (3) the brain organizes in a use-dependent fashion—if parts of the brain go unused (are not stimulated by the environment), they will not be organized in a mature, functional way, and neural development will be disrupted; and (4) the brain develops via windows of opportunity and windows of vulnerability. There are times during development when one neural system is more sensitive to experiences than others.

Both genetics and environment play key roles in the neurodevelopment of the mature brain. Perry (2002) summarized the eight major processes that occur in development (see table 2.1).

There is no single process in brain development that is more important than any other. They all need to occur for a mature, structured, organized brain that can function at a high level. The neurodevelopmental sensitivity evident in each of these processes does allow significant developmental advances in response to predictable, nurturing, repetitive, and

Table 2.1. Major Processes of Brain Development

Brain process	Description
Neurogenesis	The "birth" of neurons, most occurring during the 2nd and 3rd trimesters in utero. At birth, the majority of neurons that we will use throughout our lifetime are present. By age 5, the total volume of the brain is about 90% of adult size.
Migration	As neurons are born and the brain grows, neurons move to different parts of the brain to perform different functions
Differentiation	Neurons specialize during development to create a unique neurochemistry, neuroarchitecture, and functional capability. Each of these differentiating "choices" are the product of the intensity, pattern, and timing of environmental experiences.
Adoptosis	During development, redundant or under-activated neurons die. Neurons that make synaptic connections with others and have an adequate level of activation will survive; neurons with little activity resorb (i.e., use it or lose it).
Aborization	As neurons differentiate they send out fiber-like processes called dendrites. The more frequent, intense, and complex the incoming signals (experiences), the more dense and connected the dendrite becomes.
Synaptogenesis	Developing neurons also send out fiber-like processes that become synapses and axons. Synapses are the connections that allow neurons to communicate with each other, which they do primarily via chemical neurotransmitters.
Synaptic sculpting	Synapses that are actively used will be strengthened, making communication between neurons more efficient. When there is little activity, the synaptic connection will dissolve.
Myelination	Specialized glial cells wrap around axons creating more efficient electrochemical transduction down the neuron. This allows a neural network to function more rapidly and efficiently, allowing more complex functioning. The process of myelination continues in many key areas throughout childhood with a final burst in key cortical areas taking place during adolescence.

Source: Perry, B. (2002). Childhood experience and the expression of genetic potential: What childhood neglect tells us about nature and nurture. Brain and Mind, 3, 1.

enriching experiences, but it also makes the developing child vulnerable to adverse experiences that are unpredictable, harsh, and repetitive in a negative way (e.g., exposure to violence, neglect). While there exists some controversy over whether brain development is affected by short critical periods in development or by longer periods of developmental sensitivity, it is clear that particular environmental influences at different times in development can significantly affect the development and function of the brain.[5] For example, the first few years of life are extremely sensitive to the quality of a child's attachment bonds to a caregiver and to a child's ability to form emotionally mature relationships with others. If positive attachments are not formed early on, this does not mean that a child will be unable to form attachments to others later in life (e.g., adolescence and young adulthood), but difficulties with early attachment—being in a neglectful, aversive environment—will make forming later attachments much more difficult.

Various functions and behaviors are controlled by different parts of the brain. This makes sense if we follow the sequential model of development. The core or basic areas of the brain develop first, and these control the more simple regulatory processes like breathing, heart rate, blood pressure, and body temperature. These basic human functions are controlled mostly by the brainstem and midbrain areas of the brain. Next to develop are the upper parts of the brain, including the limbic and cortical areas. These control more complex functions like language and abstract thought. Generally, different parts of the brain mature in a very specific order (from simple to more complex), but how thoroughly each area of the brain develops depends on how much the area is used and whether environmental or genetic insults occur when that part of the brain is most sensitive to development. Perry (1997) asserts that the relationship between the primitive portions of the brain and the higher-functioning areas is key to understanding the neurobiology of violence.[6] If an individual experiences factors that increase the activity of the basic areas of the brain (e.g., chronic violence or trauma) or experience factors that decrease the ability of the higher-functioning areas of the brain to limit the natural impulsiveness of the lower brain functions (e.g., abuse/neglect, alcohol use), that person will show an increased capacity for aggression, impulsivity, and violence.

Sensory experiences are critical for teaching brain cells their jobs, and after the early critical periods of development, brain cells lose the opportunity to learn those jobs. Both human and animal research studies show that different types of environmental experiences and stimuli (e.g., neglect) affect the development of very specific parts of the brain that control such outcomes as emotion, aggression, violence, problem solving, learning, and language.[7] Infancy and early childhood is when the core neurobiological organization of individuals occurs, mostly via brain development, and this neurobiological maturation is significantly affected by the type, intensity, and quality of attachments and relationships with caretakers.

When a child experiences environmental stress, affected hormones such as cortisol, adrenaline, and serotonin alter the brain's chemistry in negative ways, increasing risk for aggression, poor impulse control, and depression, and lessening the chances for resilience and coping. For example, laboratory studies with animals show that exposure to stress hormones causes the connections between brain cells to shrivel up, and prolonged exposure actually kills the cells, particularly in the regions of the brain responsible for learning and memory. Higher levels of stress hormone are also related to increased rates of depression, withdrawal, and aggression among young children.[8]

Does the Brain Continue to Develop through Adolescence?

Our increased understanding of the development of brain structure and chemistry comes from recent technological advances in brain imaging techniques such as magnetic resonance imaging (MRI) and functional MRIs that assess the flow of oxygen to different parts of the brain based on the level of activity that is occurring there under specific conditions. We also have increased our capacity with computer aided tomography (CAT) scans of the brain to examine size, injury, and functioning. Scientists have also developed techniques to track the development of white matter (myelinized neurons) in the brain, something called diffusion tensor imaging (DTI), that quantifies the way water molecules are diffused in different regions of the brain.[9] What we know about the brain and how it develops is changing regularly and will continue to expand how we view overall child development. Changes in science and technology will also continue to affect our understanding of how biology, genes, and environment interact to influence child behavior, emotions, and mental health.

There exists some evidence that, while the majority of brain growth and development occurs during the first few years of life, the brain is not completely done growing, changing, and adapting to environmental influences. For example, Geidd and colleagues (1999)[10] found that from age four through the early twenties, the brain continues to experience noticeable growth in white matter with a corresponding decrease in gray matter. White matter is made up of myelinated neurons (suggesting they have been actively used), whereas gray matter is made up of neural cells that have not been myelinated. Some studies have further pinpointed bursts in white matter growth during adolescence, particularly in the front part of the brain, which is associated with higher-order cognitive functions like efficiency in processing information and ability to solve complex problems.[11] A recent review of adolescent brain development and vulnerability to substance-use addiction points out that significant changes in the circuitry, anatomy, and function of the brain during adolescence may place youth at heightened risk for substance-use disorders during this phase of development, sort of like a critical period of susceptibility.[12]

In another study using sophisticated imaging techniques, Chung and colleagues showed in a small sample of early adolescents (ages twelve to sixteen) increased folding in the neural tissues in the frontal lobe part of the brain, a kind of cortical thickening process.[13] They interpret this finding as evidence of the brain's constant changing to increase efficiency. In the same study, they also found increases in the size of the corpus callosum, which serves as the main link between the right and left hemispheres of the brain. If increased size is related to increased functioning, then this change in the brain may reflect an increase in the brain's ability to go back and forth between left and right sides to learn more complex and analytical information (right side) and then apply this in more flexible, creative ways to solve problems (left side).

Can We Settle the Nature vs. Nurture Debate?

One of the most significant historical debates in the social sciences is the relative influence of genetics versus environment on individual growth and development. Is it genetics that predicts our personalities, or is it the way we are raised by our parents or other significant adults? Most people believe that the way we raise our children has an effect on how they turn out as adolescents and adults. We believe that if we put forth the effort to be consistent, warm, supportive, and nurturing, our children will grow up to be caring, responsible, productive citizens. It's not easy, and there is not a clear formula for success. We all recognize that many factors can impact the socialization and developmental process. We have repeatedly studied many different factors over the years to see if they have an effect on child development. We study parenting styles, parent IQ, and education levels. We examine the influence of poverty and social class on child academic achievement and school readiness. We have spent years trying to understand the influence of divorce on child outcomes and whether growing up in a single-parent family really places a child at risk for more problem outcomes later in life compared to children who grow up in "intact" (i.e., two-parent) families.

Some of the things we study we cannot change. One cannot easily change a child's gender or ethnicity. A child's body type, how tall or athletic a child is, or whether a youngster has severe acne are all physical characteristics that are very difficult to change via environmental interventions. We know that improvements in nutrition have lead to the earlier onset of puberty among adolescents in Western countries, so there is some evidence that environmental or cultural shifts can impact child outcomes, even those that have a significant physical or genetic basis to them.

Recently, several well-respected works have questioned the notion that socialization has as much impact on child development and personality as we once thought. Judith Harris wrote about the influence of genetics versus environment in her compelling book *The Nurture Assumption*.[14] She argues that personality is largely due to genetics and that social factors (parenting, peers, quality of education) have a much smaller impact on these genetic predispositions. David Rowe, in his book *The Limits of Family Influence*, thoroughly reviews social science research and concludes that, with the exception of some extreme family-environment situations such as child abuse and neglect or those that are devoid of opportunity, broad differences in family environments exert little influence on personality development over the life course.[15]

Rowe bases this conclusion largely on a review of the most scientifically rigorous behavior-genetic studies of intelligence, personality, and psychopathology. The typical behavior-genetic study involves assessing some construct like intelligence in samples of twins, particularly identical twins who are raised apart. This is the most ideal situation for a study of the relative influence of genes versus environment because identical twins (as compared to fraternal twins) share the same genetic makeup. Taking the position that socialization is what matters, if two identical twins grow up in separate families and have very different cultural experiences over time, one would expect that as adolescents or adults, these two individuals would be markedly different, at least as different as their family experiences and cultures would suggest. While they might physically look the same (because they are genetically the same), they might have different personalities because one family was strict while the other was laissez-faire, or one family was Catholic while the other was Muslim, or one child attended a private school in an affluent suburb while the other attended an inner-city public school. In the end, however, when one thoroughly examines the well-designed (i.e., rigorously conducted) behavior-genetic studies of child outcomes, the evidence suggests that what we inherit genetically from our biological parents has more influence on who we are and what we become than all of the socialization influences combined.

This is not to say that environments and socialization play no role, and in fact the evidence largely suggests that *both* genes and environment predict child outcomes. Some researchers theorize that most of us are predisposed to certain things like illness to varying degrees, but only some of us experience the illness based on the timing, type, or intensity of our exposure to various things in our environments. For example, we may all be predisposed to becoming depressed to different degrees, but only some of us will become clinically depressed, or depressed enough that we may need medication to help stabilize our mood. People with a low threshold or tolerance may become depressed easily whenever they are faced with unexpected stress across their lives. Other individuals may have a higher tolerance for stress and may occasionally be moody, but they may never have a significant problem with being depressed chronically over time. The same rationale applies to certain extreme illnesses like schizophrenia. Some theories postulate that we are all disposed to developing schizophrenia under the right circumstances, but if individuals experience a traumatic event at the wrong time, they are more likely to develop a thought disorder than if they hadn't gone through that experience. Of course, we also know a lot about the risk for illnesses like cancer and bipolar disorder simply by knowing whether our parents or grandparents also suffered from the disorder.

A very recent study showed how family environment can moderate the influence of genes on alcoholism. A team lead by Ted Jacob of the Palo Alto Veterans Affairs Health Care System looked at sets of identical male twins in which one twin was an alcoholic and one was not. The study found that children raised by the alcoholic twin were twice as likely to develop alcoholism as the children raised by the genetically identical twin who was not an alcoholic. In other words, children who were at high genetic risk of alcoholism but who were raised by the nonalcoholic twin father had only about the same risk of developing the disease as children in the control group did (those in families not raised by any of the twin fathers, alcoholics and nonalcoholics). What this finding suggests is that environmental influences in general, and family environment in particular, can have a significant impact on preventing alcoholism, even in children at the same genetically high risk of developing the disorder. The role of environmental factors like parental modeling of drinking behavior and high-conflict family environments (that often lead to drinking as a coping mechanism) should be taken into account when trying to understand disorders with a strong genetic basis.

What does all this have to do with violence and mental health? Well, for starters, it is clear that genetics plays a significant role in determining our risk for developing violent behavior and mental health problems. Given their genetic load, individuals can then be at more or less risk depending on their environment and socialization experiences. If we grow up in a supportive, loving environment where we experience few stressors, we may minimize our risk for developing significant mental health problems. If, on the other hand, we grow up in an unstable, rejecting, violent environment, we may significantly increase our risk for mental health and behavior-problem outcomes even if our biological risk for developing mental health problems is low. Of course, there are also plenty of examples where children have grown up in seemingly supportive, loving environments with lots of opportunities, but they still experience significant problems in adolescence and young adulthood. One type of environmental risk factor that we consider in this book is the impact of violence on a child's behavior and mental health.

Genes and Depression

Recently, researchers have identified some specific links between genes and mental health. For example, Caspi and his colleagues have identified a single gene that seems to help determine why some people get depressed in response to stress.[16] The gene is for a chemical transporter called 5-HTT, which handles transmission of the neurotransmitter serotonin, most often associated with mood and depression. This relatively common gene comes in two forms, a long form and a short form. The researchers surveyed young adults, ages twenty-one to twenty-six, about stressful life events such as romantic breakups, illnesses, job crises, and bereavements, and they also asked respondents about whether they had been depressed or suicidal in the past year. For people who did not report any major life stressors, the probability of being depressed was the same regardless of the form of the 5-HTT gene they had. However, for people who did report major life stressors, the probability of also being depressed was much higher for those with short forms of the gene than for those with long forms of the gene. For example, the average score on a depression survey was more than twice as high for stressed people with two short forms of the gene than for people who had two long forms of the gene. In a related finding, the team also found that experiencing abuse as a child predicted depression after the age of eighteen only in people with the short form of the gene. Among the 11 percent of individuals who reported experiencing severe maltreatment as children, the subjects with two short forms of the gene ran a 63 percent risk of a major depressive episode. People with the long version of the 5-HTT gene averaged a 30 percent risk for depression, regardless of whether they had been abused as children.

These findings are consistent with animal studies of the 5-HTT gene that found animals with two long forms of the gene cope better in stressful conditions than do those with short forms of the gene. Other studies of humans show that people with short forms of the 5-HTT allele show more intense brain reactions to fearful stimuli than do those without this version.[17] Previous work in the 1990s showed a weak link between short forms of this gene and neuroticism as a personality trait (sort of the Woody Allen gene). It seems that people with long forms of the gene are more emotionally resilient and more likely to go with the flow when faced with a stressful situation, whereas those with short forms of the gene take things much more seriously and are much more likely to feel stressed out and unable to cope with unexpected, stressful events. This combination of studies is a very good example of work that attempts to document how the interplay between genes and environmental influences has an effect on behavior and mental health.

Is vulnerability to depression normal? Seventy percent of us have at least one short 5-HTT gene, so if being normal means most of us have it, then depression does seem to be normal. But not everyone with the genes becomes depressed, so this must mean that environment, at some level, plays a role. If someone is predisposed genetically to depression, Caspi's work and others' shows that early trauma and adversity (in this case, severe maltreatment or victimization from violence) lead to depressive symptoms and subsequent changes in the brain. Chronic depression produces more marked changes. Particular brain regions begin to shrink or show structural disorganization. Does having the 5-HTT gene in long form help to somehow repair the brain or stop its damage? The answers to these questions remain for future research, but the early findings from animal and human studies show a clear link between genes that affect mental health and environmental experiences that impact whether and how those genes are expressed in everyday life. For example, the most recent research on the brain shows that decreased levels of serotonin (5-HTT) are associated with increased impulsive behavior, suicide, and even fire starting.[18]

Another main hormone involved in regulating emotions (and therefore mental health) and the propensity for aggression and violence is dopamine. Dopamine is most widely known, perhaps, for its role in the regulation of symptoms related to Parkinson's disease. In some parts of the brain dopamine regulates emotion, while in other parts of the brain it regulates motor movement. We've known for some time, for example, that individuals who suffer from Parkinson's have lower levels of dopamine in their brains than normal. Dopamine plays a role in motivation and in how we learn new behaviors. Increased levels of dopamine have been associated with the pharmacological action of many different types of addictive drugs like nicotine, alcohol, cocaine, and amphetamines, as well as with the reward we experience naturally through food and sex, or artificially through video games. The release of dopamine has also been associated with the experience of stressful or aversive stimuli, like violence.[19]

Is there a link between depression and violence? There is some evidence that the children of mothers who were depressed postpartum (after the child is born) are at significantly increased risk for engaging in violent behavior later in life.[20] One prominent theory is that depressed mothers have difficulty interacting with their infants and young toddlers, and these difficulties translate into problems later on for the child in regulating emotions and attention. Developmentally, learning how to regulate emotion and attention are important normative tasks of infancy and toddlerhood, and having a depressed mother during this time seems to disrupt the process. When a depressed mother is less able to respond contingently to her baby (e.g., when the baby cries, the mother responds), both mother and baby become distressed, and, because infants cannot depend on mom to respond to their cries, their distress persists, making it harder for them to learn how to self-regulate. Recently, researchers found that risk for violence at age eleven was greatest in the group of children whose mothers were depressed during the postpartum period (at three months) and at least once thereafter.[21] These children were more likely to use weapons and to engage in frequent fighting at school (by teacher report) compared to other children.

Experiencing Trauma

Years ago, I was riding on a plane from Cleveland to Tucson, Arizona. We lived in Tucson and had gone home to visit family for Thanksgiving. We were on our way back to the southwest on a clear, sunny day, traveling with our oldest son Joseph, who was about three months old at the time. Back then, you didn't have to purchase an extra seat for an infant, so he rode with my wife and I, and she was holding him in her lap. About twenty minutes into the flight, as I was reading my newspaper, the pilot came on over the intercom and said something like, "I'm sorry to have to tell you this, but we are experiencing problems with the plane's hydraulic system, and we've lost the ability to steer the airplane. We have to prepare for an immediate emergency landing. Please take everything out of your pockets and place your head between your knees."

Suffice it say that people on the plane did not take this sudden news very well. There was some initial screaming, but that quickly subsided to mumbling and some crying as the flight attendants came around giving instructions to passengers and reassuring them that everything was going to be OK. I remember the flight attendant who came by our seat and placed her hand on my shoulder. She was smiling, which was mildly reassuring. I also noticed she was very pregnant, because by now I was holding my son tightly in my lap. After a few words of general encouragement directed at no one—"Everything will be all right. This is no big deal; it's happened to me before" (I'm not sure if that was encouraging or not, but I appreciated the effort)—she leaned over to me and said, loud enough for my wife to hear sitting beside me, "You know, you're sitting right over the wheels, and because we've lost hydraulic power, we don't know if the wheels will come down or not when we try to land. And, if they do come down, we're not really sure they'll stay down. So, as soon as we hit ground, there might be lots of fire, so I want you to look out your window at the wings and see how much fire there is before you try to get out."

Well, this didn't sit too well with my wife, and my own level of anxiety began to quickly rise. My heart began beating faster. My palms got sweaty. I remember the complete feeling of helplessness. There was nothing I could do but hope that the pilots would somehow figure out how to land the plane safely. My wife was crying. My son was crying. The young man behind me leaned forward and gave me his suit jacket. "Here, take this to cushion the baby's head," he said. This was a small act of kindness at a trying time that I will never forget. My wife kept repeating, "It can't end this way," and I kept trying to reassure her that it wouldn't. We did a quick life review with each other and, I'm sure, to ourselves.

The ending of the story is a happy one. Obviously, I'm still here and able to write about it years later. After flying around for a while, our plane was diverted to a large airport because, as we were told, it had more emergency response equipment (again, I'm not sure if that was meant to make us feel better or upset us more). As we came in for our landing, I remember looking out the window at all the fire trucks racing down the runway along with us. I also remember looking for flames, and, much to my relief, I didn't see any. I remember holding tight to my son and rocking him gently in our seat, trying not to crush him out of adrenaline, tension, and fear. I remember my wife holding onto my arm so hard that I had bruises for days. The best thing I remember is finally coming to a stop. We careened off the runway into a muddy field, and everyone on the plane immediately began to cheer.

While the incident on the plane had a happy ending, I remember it to this day, ten years later, as if it happened yesterday. I also think about it every time I get on a plane or hear about a plane crashing. For me, the PTSD symptoms persist, manifested in becoming more anxious when I fly. I have to constantly reassure myself and tell myself out loud that thousands of planes take off and land every day without incident. I have to work hard to convince myself every time that nothing bad will happen, that incidents are very unusual and rare, and that people fly all the time without ever experiencing anything even close to what happened to us. I have to remind myself that even with all the bad that could have happened, we landed safely. It is this self-talk and rationalization that helps me get back on the plane each time, that helps me cope every time the plane I'm on lurches in turbulence. I have to keep busy on a plane, reading or working, to keep my mind off what happened. The one problem with that strategy is that I was reading a newspaper at the time we found out we were in trouble, so literally every time I pick up a newspaper to read on the plane, I think about that moment, even briefly, and I have to tell myself that things will be OK. I still fly regularly, and it does seem to get a little easier with each flight that I get on and off without incident.

My wife, on the other hand, refuses to fly alone and generally avoids flying on a plane. It is still too anxiety provoking for her to fly. We don't go on family vacations that require us to all fly in a plane together. Over time, she has lost sleep, and we've both had occasional nightmares about what happened. These, too, have become less frequent and intense as time has gone by, but the memories linger. We both get tense for several days before I leave on a flight. I'm sure part of it is knowing what could happen on a plane and the intense feelings of helplessness we had on that day that we still carry with us.

I thought about my experience that day when the events of 9-11 were unfolding, and I thought about how the people on those planes must have felt once they knew they were in danger, about how they must have felt helpless about what was happening to them, perhaps going through their own sense of anxiety and fear, completing their own life reviews in their heads, and holding on tightly to the person seated next to them. For those who figured out what was going on and took action, the end was much less positive than it was for us. The point is that in response to any traumatic or violent event, our bodies and minds respond in a very specific physiological way, and emotionally we can be affected in a significant way, sometimes to the point that we actually experience post-traumatic stress disorder syndrome. PTSD is discussed in more detail later, but let's first review what happens to the brain in response to stress or fear, and how brain development can be affected by violence.

How the Brain Reacts to Fear: Stressing Out

The developing brain makes children especially vulnerable to emotional experiences. When these experiences are unpredictable, intense, and get repeated over time, the brain's structure and chemistry can be permanently altered. When individuals are anxious or under stress, we know that they eat more, they drink more, and they get into more accidents. People who are under a lot of stress have more trouble sleeping, they're more cranky and irritable, and they experience more conflict in their relationships with others. Recent research also tells us that an individual's immune system is compromised by stress, making the person more susceptible to illnesses as common as a cold or as serious as a heart attack.

What happens biologically when we are exposed to stress, trauma, or violence? I remember in college I took a woman to a movie on a date. It was not a bad plan, except the movie was *A Clockwork Orange* by Stanley Kubrick. Given that it was the mid–1980s, the movie had been out a while, but I was naive and did not know much about it. Suffice it say, this is not a good date movie. Very early in the movie, there occurs a violent rape scene. By any standards, it is not a very pleasant thing to watch. How do most of us react when we are exposed to something very violent and uncomfortable? Our hearts race, we get nervous and fidgety, our palms get a little sweaty, and we want to get out of the situation, to avoid or escape from the unpleasantness we are experiencing. This is referred to as the fight-or-flight response to stress. Beat it and get over it, or get away from it.

Fear and anxiety are normal instincts rooted in our biological responses to stress and trauma. They are survival instincts. One particularly cool night in Tucson, my wife and I were returning from a get-together at a friend's house. We lived in an apartment in the foothills of the surrounding mountains. As we approached the entry gate to our building, we were startled to find that a mountain lion had crawled onto the hood of a car just outside the gate. Of course we were used to seeing javelinas (wild boars) once in a while, and even the occasional scorpion or desert wolf, but never had we confronted a mountain lion. As you might expect, this generated a brief bout of anxiety and fear, and our natural reaction was to quickly make our way to another entrance, away from the potential threat. Escape and avoidance helped ensure our survival, which would have been less likely an outcome if my wife had approached the lion and yelled frantically to try and scare it away (nothing she would ever admit to having tried, of course).

How does the brain respond to stress, anxiety, and fear? A good place to start is with the anatomy of fear.[22] The most important part of the brain relative to understanding fear and violence is the amygdala, a small almond-shaped structure in the center of the brain (part of the lower brain that forms first in the sequence of development) that is connected to other critical parts of the brain through nerve fibers. The amygdala serves as the brain's rapid-response system and is automatically triggered (even unconsciously) when we perceive a threat in our environment. Cowley (2003) describes the amygdala's response:

> Once it perceives a threat, it can trigger a body-wide emergency response within milliseconds. Jolted by impulses from the amygdala, the nearby hypothalamus produces a hormone called corticotrophin releasing factor, or CRF, which signals the pituitary and adrenal glands to flood the bloodstream with epinephrine (adrenaline), norepinephrine, and cortisol. Those stress hormones then shut down nonemergency services such as digestion and immunity, and direct the body's resources to fighting or fleeing. The heart pounds, the lungs pump, and muscles get an energizing blast of glucose. The stress hormones also act on the brain, creating a state of heightened alertness and supercharging the circuitry involved in memory formation. (p. 46)

In essence, the brain makes a memory of the stress-producing event, and every time a similar stressful or anxiety-producing event occurs (e.g., chronic exposure to violence), the memory is reinforced, sort of like being etched on the brain.

Cowley (2003) goes on to summarize what we know about the impact of chronic stress on the brain and the body:

> Acute fear is not the only kind that can hurt you. Constant, low-grade adrenaline baths may subtly damage the heart, raising the long-term risk of cardiovascular disease. Continuous exposure to cortisol can dampen the immune system, leaving stressed people more vulnerable to infections and possibly even cancer. Stress hormones can harm the brain, too, severing connections among neurons. In both human and animal studies, researchers have found that prolonged stress also shrinks the hippocampus, a brain structure that plays critical roles in processing and storing information. (p. 47–48)

The evidence is pretty clear. The neurochemistry, functioning, and very structure of the brain is significantly impacted by trauma, fear, anxiety, and stress. Many of the neurochemicals and hormones involved in the brain's response to stress and fear are the same as those involved in maintaining our mental health and determining whether we are aggressive and impulsive or passive and restrained.

Exposure to Violence Affects Our Brain

When a child experiences adversity in the form of exposure to violence and trauma or victimization from violence, there can be significant disruptions in the development of the brain, and the physical structure of the way the brain operates can change. It is particularly important to understand the timing of adversity with respect to the developing brain. If significant changes in neurochemistry and structure occur early and are due to chronic stress over time, it is more likely that functioning later in life will be significantly impacted. The longer and more often the changes in neurochemistry and structure are reinforced over time (due to repeated exposure to violence, stressors, or reexperiencing the trauma), the more difficult it will be to change those brain responses to the environment in the future.

In addition to the brain's response to trauma and stress outlined above, there has been specific research on how exposure to violence can affect a child's brain chemistry and structure and on the resulting difficulties in behavior and learning. We know, for example, that children exposed to high levels of violence or who are chronically exposed to violence become hypervigilant, easily aroused by things going on in the environment around them. They become desensitized to violence and respond to exposure without empathy or concern for the impact that violence has on others. Studies of young children and adolescents exposed to chronic violence show that exposure results in a lower resting heart rate as opposed to the increased heart rate most of us experience when we are exposed to violent stimuli.

Early Neglect

Studies with animals have also told us a great deal about how the brain develops and how it is affected by early neglect and deprivation. In general, the brains of animals raised in deprived conditions are smaller, less complex in their structure, and less flexible in their functioning than the brains of animals reared in more enriched environments. Animals raised in stimulating, enriched environments also have higher-density brains, usually reflecting more neurons and synapses, than do animals raised in deprived settings.

Studies of human infants confirm much of these findings from animal studies. Some of the most significant early work was conducted by Spitz with children reared in large orphanages. Historically, some orphanages were characterized as environments that did not provide much individual stimulation, individual attention, or emotional affection. While an infant's basic needs were generally met via food and clothing, not much else was going on between child and caregiver. With respect to brain development, these were fairly neglectful, deprived settings. What Spitz and others have since found was that once children from these institutional settings were placed in more enriching, stimulating environments such as foster homes with nurturing adults, they experienced significant gains in their cognitive functioning, physical development, and social and emotional functioning. The longer a child is in a neglectful, deprived environment, the lower the level of recovery of skills and functioning. For example, some studies have shown that if children are adopted to a home before the age of six months, they experience even more positive future gains than do children adopted between six months and two years of age, but all children adopted before the age of two do better over time than do children adopted at older ages. In short, the earlier children get into a nourishing, stimulating, and supportive environment, the better they do in the long run with respect to how they function and develop cognitively, socially, physically, and emotionally.

Part of predicting how a child will do over time has to do with how the brain is affected by early chronic neglect and social/emotional deprivation. Many children who suffer from neglect show abnormal brain-scan results on MRI and CAT scans. If children are removed from neglectful settings, they show some recovery of brain size and functioning. As Perry (2002) summarizes, "The human cortex grows in size, develops complexity, makes synaptic connections and modifies as a function of the quality and quantity of sensory experience. Sensory-motor and cognitive deprivation leads to underdevelopment in the cortex in rats, non-human primates and humans."[23]

The clear implication of all of this is that early life experiences, particularly the relationship formed between infant and primary caregiver, are significantly important to determining how the mature brain will be organized, how it will function, and how it will react to stress. Our ability to form relationships with others, our ability to tolerate frustration, and our ability to resolve problems without being aggressive and impulsive, all of these outcomes depend in part on early brain maturation and the quality of early relationships with significant adults.

CHAPTER THREE

ARE CHILDREN BORN VIOLENT OR DO WE JUST MAKE THEM THAT WAY?

The way to start understanding violence is to place it in the context of development. Violence occurs along a developmental continuum, manifesting itself differently from early childhood through adolescence and into adulthood. Being exposed to violence over time as a child has a significant impact on how one views the world, and it affects whether or not an individual is able to cope with problems in everyday life; how an individual handles unexpected crises (death, accidents, injuries, terrorism, natural disasters, and so on); and whether children are able to realize their full potential as individuals.

Figure 3.1 illustrates the many factors that can contribute to violent, delinquent behavior in adolescence.[1] Some of the risk factors related to later violent behavior are present even before birth. For example, children do not decide which families they are born into. When a child is born into a family that has a history of violence across generations, that child is at greater risk of learning, from a very early age, that violence and aggression are the normal ways people interact with each other. A child born into a violent family is more likely to be exposed, chronically over time, to many different types of violence on a daily basis. A child born into a family that views violence as a culturally acceptable way of disciplining is likely to learn to deal with others through the use of force, power, and control. A child born into a family whose religious beliefs support the use of aggression and violence in discipline or family relationships is more likely to grow up believing that these are morally acceptable means of behaving toward others.

45

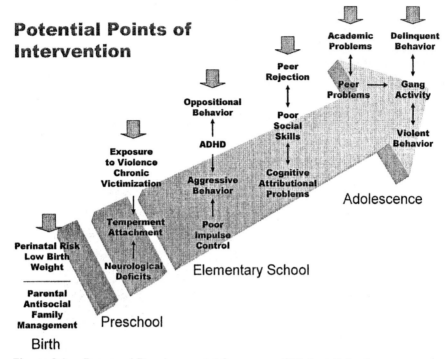

Figure 3.1.   Proposed Developmental Sequence of Violent Behavior.
Source: Daniel J. Flannery (1997), *School Violence: Risk, Prevention, and Policy*, ERIC Clearinghouse on Urban Education, Urban Diversity Series No. 109.

Children also have no control over what they are exposed to as a developing fetus or what happens to them at birth. We know that children born small for their gestational age or with a very low birth weight are more likely to have difficulty in multiple domains as they grow up, especially with respect to learning, academic achievement, and problem solving,[2] placing them at greater risk for subsequent delinquency and violence in adolescence and young adulthood. Children who are deprived of oxygen at birth are more likely to experience complications related to learning disabilities and school dropout, risk factors that are indirectly related to an increased likelihood of delinquency and violence.

As a child matures through infancy and toddlerhood, we can often see signs of personality and temperament that may increase risk for violence. For example, some children when faced with adversity seem to be readily able to go with the flow, shift gears, and attack the problem from a new angle. Other children are easily frustrated, find it difficult to adapt to changing situations, and are impulsive in their thinking and in their behavior. We will discuss resiliency and social competence in greater detail later. Attachment also plays a significant role in risk for aggression, delinquency, and violence. A child who is unable to form a secure attachment with a primary caregiver or other significant adult will experience more difficulty later in life in forming meaningful, supportive relationships with others, and as an adolescent will have difficulty developing mature relationships with peers and may struggle to form a clear sense of identity and independence.

As you will hear about throughout this book, children exposed to violence from an early age, especially those victimized by violence or chronically exposed to violence, are at significantly greater risk of perpetrating violence themselves as they grow older. In fact, there has been significant research on the cycle of violence, and we know that if a child is victimized by violence or directly witnesses a significant amount of violence when young, the child's risk of eventually becoming a perpetrator of violence increases by as much as 40 percent.

Figure 3.1 also illustrates a number of key points about the development of violent behavior from infancy through adolescence. First, there are many factors that increase risk for these poor outcomes, but there exists no single pathway to predicting who will become violent or gang involved and who will not. These risk factors interact with each other in sometimes very complex ways, and they affect different individuals in different ways depending on genetics, environment, timing, opportunity, and the resources individuals have available to them (both internally and externally) to deal with these factors. We know that the more risk factors there are present, the higher the likelihood of a negative outcome, and that the earlier the risk factors begin to operate, the higher the likelihood of negative outcomes. Timing matters, intensity matters, and chronicity matters.

Finally, figure 3.1 illustrates that there are several choice points for intervention along the developmental continuum of factors that contribute to risk for delinquency and violence. The longer we wait to intervene with prevention or treatment, the longer we allow the constellation of risk factors to operate and compound their potential effects. It's like cancer. Early

detection and treatment are much more effective in preventing the outcome (death) than is waiting until the cancer gets really bad before we intervene. Unfortunately, our juvenile justice system and schools are
generally set up to act in the latter scenario: wait to intervene until the behavior becomes very serious or disruptive (e.g., a child drops out of school
permanently or perpetrates a serious act of delinquency or violence) and
then take action. Of course at this point the cost of intervention is much
higher, the intensity of intervention required to make a difference is much
greater, and the chance of failing to make a difference is much more likely
than if we had identified the problems earlier and had intervened in a preventive way when a child was much younger.

There are many factors that interact with each other to increase the
risk of adolescent violence, delinquent behavior, and gang involvement.
For example, youth with significant learning difficulties or attention problems are much more likely to drop out of school early than are other children. Level of academic achievement is significantly related to adult
outcomes like employment, quality of life, and job satisfaction, with school
dropouts (those dropping out of school before completing elementary or
high school) earning significantly less; being less satisfied with their lives
in general; being less healthy; and being more likely to experience marital
conflict, divorce, incarceration, and substance-use problems than do individuals who complete higher levels of education (e.g., who graduate from
college). Delinquency, crime, and recidivism are also directly related to
level of educational attainment. Youth who drop out of school are more
likely to hang out with other youth who have also dropped out of school.
With few opportunities for employment or income generation, and with
little adult supervision, these youth are much more likely to engage in
delinquent behavior, substance use, early sexual activity, and crime. The
earlier this cycle of school dropout and delinquent behavior begins, the
more likely it is that it will lead to a persistent pattern of conduct problems and to poor adult outcomes.

Developmental Pathways to Violence

Of all the risk factors identified for placing a child at risk for adolescent
violence (and delinquency, conduct disorder, and antisocial behavior), high
aggressive behavior in childhood is the most significant. However, not all

children who are aggressive grow up to become delinquent, violent adolescents. Over time, some children appear to be desisters (start but eventually stop), while others are persisters (start and keep going, usually getting worse). Still others appear to be late starters, not engaging in any serious delinquent or violent behavior until adolescence and young adulthood. So what are the various pathways and combinations of risk factors that tell us which child is most at risk for ending up as the delinquent, violent, maybe gang-involved adolescent?

With the emergence of findings from several long-term studies, some up to thirty years long, we are beginning to get a clearer picture of the developmental course of aggressive behavior as it contributes to later conduct disorder, antisocial behavior, criminal involvement, and violence. There currently exist at least three separate models of the developmental trajectories followed toward later antisocial outcomes. The first model identifies three pathways that lead to different types of delinquency and criminal involvement.[3] This is the *overt pathway*, wherein high levels of aggression in childhood precede adolescent violence. This is the pathway we're most familiar with, because the aggressive preschooler who does poorly in school, constantly gets into fights with peers, and has trouble getting along with teachers (even as early as in kindergarten or first grade) is the most easily identifiable problem child. The second is the *covert pathway*, where covert antisocial acts in childhood lead to nonviolent, property-oriented crimes in adolescence and young adulthood. This is distinctly different from the first pathway in that antisocial behavior in the covert pathway does not involve confrontation or interaction with another person. The third pathway is the *authority conflict pathway*, characterized by an oppositional, defiant, stubborn child who defies authority figures, engages in deviance, and grows up to engage in later status offending, which is a less serious form of offending than violent, antisocial behavior.

An alternative theory posited by Patterson and colleagues in the late 1980s suggests that adult criminal behavior results from two distinct paths.[4] An individual can either be an *early starter* on the pathway or a *late starter*. An early starter grows up in a family characterized by coercive parent-child interactions, engages in problem behavior early in childhood, and experiences school failure at an early age. The late starter, the theory goes, does not have the longstanding history of family, behavior, and academic problems of the early starter, but begins engaging in delinquent, antisocial, or violent behavior for the first time in early adolescence. Reasons for this late start include hanging out with deviant peers who are prone to getting into trouble, having parents who are poor monitors of their child's behavior, and oppositional and defiant behavior that may be related to increased conflict with parents and strivings for independence and autonomy.

Expanding on much of the research done by Patterson's team, Terri Moffit and her colleagues, who have conducted a great deal of cutting-edge research of their own, expanded on Patterson's model but also proposed two mutually exclusive groups of antisocial youth.[5] The first are the *life-course-persistent* offenders. These youth begin early and engage in high levels of aggressive behavior consistently over time, escalating the seriousness of their behavior as they mature through childhood and adolescence and into adulthood. The life-course-persistent offenders continue to perpetrate violence as adults and are most likely to end up incarcerated or dead as a result of their violent, offending behavior. The second distinct group is the *adolescence-limited* offenders who engage in nonviolent forms of antisocial behavior, but only during the adolescent years.

Aspects of all three of these theories about the developmental trajectory of aggression and violence have received significant support in the scientific literature, from survey studies of specific groups of youth at one point in time, to more extensive and intensive longitudinal studies of youth over many years. There are, of course, many variations on these basic themes of development, some taking school failure into greater account, others highlighting the role of genes and personality as core risk factors intensified by specific environmental experiences. Some theories posit unique trajectories for youth who have attention-deficit/hyperactivity disorder (ADHD), because this has been consistently shown to increase a child's risk for aggression, delinquency, and violence, as well as other comorbid problem behaviors like substance use and school failure.

Despite differences in the terms they use and what they emphasize, all of these theories share a common emphasis on separating out an early-onset, chronically offending group whose aggressive, violent behavior is more likely to have a genetic basis (or vulnerability) or to reflect core personality traits of the individual. Poor parenting and school failure interact with these biological, genetic factors to significantly increase the risk for antisocial, violent outcomes. There also exists a second, less severe group of individuals who start later, who typically engage in less serious forms of aggression and violence, and who are more likely to stop their offending at some point in time as they get older. Their behavior is more related to associations with deviant peers, engaging in aggression because they have the opportunity to do so (as opposed to behaving violently without empathy, remorse, or concern for the consequences), or acting out against their parents as a form of rebellion.

Of course, in all the discussion about who grows up to become violent, we shouldn't lose sight of the largest group of children: those who may engage in "developmentally appropriate" aggression and oppositional behavior (remember the terrible twos?) but who don't grow up to become aggressive, gang-involved, violent criminal offenders as adolescents and young adults.

Are Children Born Violent?

Very few of us are born to be violent. Research tells us that only about 2 to 3 percent of the population will grow up to be violent. This is the group that probably is more hardwired with the combination of genes, hormones, chemicals, and brain structure that predisposes them to become violent. They may have an aggressive, antisocial personality. They are the criminal violent offenders (or the life-course-persistent offenders, if you prefer). They start early and continue to offend, becoming more aggressive and violent as they get older. They are the John Wayne Gacys, the Jeffrey Dahmers, and the Ted Bundys of the world. They will look you straight in the eye and tell you that if you don't keep them locked up, they will go out and seriously hurt or kill again. They are among the repeat offenders, the serial rapists, the career criminals. They know no other way of behaving, and neither do they necessarily seek out alternatives to behaving in an aggressive, violent way. When given the opportunity and circumstance to offend, they will likely act in an aggressive, violent manner, no matter the consequence. Many violent offenders report that they behave impulsively, that they are unable to control their impulse or urge to hurt others or to commit a crime.

The remaining 97 percent of us, if we do behave in an aggressive, violent manner (and still, most of us don't), are essentially socialized over time to do so. It is because we grew up observing others behave this way

51

without consequence. It is because we learned, over time, that behaving aggressively was the way to influence and control others and to get our way or get what we wanted. It is because we were socialized to be assertive and aggressive to be successful and get ahead in life, but we didn't have the internal capacity or social skills to manage the aggression in socially acceptable ways. In short, for the majority of us, violence is learned behavior. We learn over time, from a multitude of social experiences, cultural experiences, and political experiences. We learn over time from what we observe at home, in the media, and on the Internet. For most of us, violence is not a random, uncontrollable, or even inevitable occurrence. The silver lining is that if violence is largely a learned behavior, then there must be ways that we can intervene effectively in the lives of young people to reduce or prevent their involvement in violence.[6] The challenge, of course, is that not all violence is of the same form or cause. What contributes to one person's aggressive, violent behavior has little or nothing to do with another person's propensity to behave violently. What's going on?

For some people, violence occurs because of factors related to specific situations or events. Situational violence has been noted under conditions of extreme heat, for example, or when individuals become frustrated because their plans are interrupted or delayed. There are many examples of violence due to road rage, when individuals who are normally not violent, per se, lose their temper and control because they are cut off in traffic or because they perceive that another driver is acting in an aggressive, disrespectful way toward them. This is a classic example of situational violence. Another example of situational violence is violence that occurs when an individual is under the influence of drugs or alcohol, or when a person uses a handgun to perpetrate violence against another person because the gun happened to be there when they were having an argument. How many times have we read about a young child who accidentally shot a playmate with a gun they found at home? These situational acts of violence are typically not planned or premeditated, and they occur when impulsive anger interacts with the circumstances of the situation. This doesn't make the outcome of the violent act any less important or less problematic, but it illustrates that not all violence has the same cause, etiology, or consequence. Estimates vary, but situational types of violence account for about 25 percent of violence among children and adolescents in the United States.

Another form of violence is relational violence, typically violence that occurs during fights or conflicts between two people who know each other. This can be two family members (e.g., a parent and a child) or two friends. This includes children who witness domestic violence between two adults in their home, sibling violence, and dating violence. All of these will be discussed in more detail later. Similar to situational violence, relational violence accounts for about one-fourth of all types of violence among children and adolescents.

The third type of violent behavior is predatory violence, which accounts for only about 5 to 8 percent of all violent acts and includes assaultive behavior, robbery and muggings, and gang related violence. Predatory violence is intentional, usually committed to obtain something or to purposely hurt someone. It is more likely to be part of a pattern of serious conduct-disordered behavior or antisocial behavior. Almost one in five adolescents report that at some point they have committed at least one act of predatory violence, but this does not mean that 20 percent of all adolescents are predatory and violent. Many theories postulate that about 8 percent of our population (of kids or adults) accounts for about 80 to 90 percent of all serious problem behavior. Most research supports this ratio of offending, criminal, violent behavior. It is true in most schools. It is true in most institutions.

The last type of violence is called psychopathological violence. It is generally more extreme than other types of violence, and it is the clearest example of individual psychopathology that is probably related to neurological deficits, brain injury, or severe psychological trauma. If violence is related to mental illness, it is usually in the form of psychopathology such as a thought disorder like schizophrenia or borderline or antisocial personality disorder. This is the type of violence most typically treated through the use of psychiatric medications, and these are the individuals most likely to end up institutionalized, if not incarcerated. Psychopathological violence is the rarest form of violence, accounting for about 1 percent of all violent behavior.

What Contributes to Predicting Violent Behavior?

In the work that my colleague Mark Singer and I have done on violence and mental health, we have also been interested in the factors that predict child and adolescent violent behavior, assessed via the behaviors mentioned earlier: hitting other children, fighting, attacking others with a knife, or shooting at someone else with a gun. There are no studies that examine every possible predictor of a behavior, but we were mostly interested in whether recent exposure to violence, defined as exposure to or victimization from violence in the past year, was a better or worse predictor of a child's violent behavior than was lifetime violence exposure, defined as witnessing or being victimized by violence in the past, not including the last year.

In a study of third through eighth graders, we examined the influence of four specific predictors of child violent behavior: parental monitoring, watching violence on television, recent exposure to violence, and past exposure to violence.[7] We examined whether these factors predicted a child's self-reported violent behavior after we took into account the influence of demographic factors like child age and gender, ethnicity, whether the child lived in a single-parent or two-parent household, and where the child lived geographically, in an urban, central city location, in a suburb, or in a rural community. We did find that males and older children, as expected, reported higher levels of violent behavior than did females and younger children. Children who reported higher levels of parental monitoring, meaning that their parents generally knew where they were and who they were with (or at least that children knew they were expected to let their parents know this) reported lower levels of violent behavior. Television-viewing habits, including how many hours of television a child watched daily and whether they preferred shows with violence and high action, were statistically related to predicting violent behavior but were substantively not very significant influences on violence.

The most significant predictor of child violent behavior was recent exposure to violence, particularly violence exposure and victimization at home and in the neighborhood. Recent exposure to violence, compared to all other factors we examined, accounted for one-fourth of the prediction of violent behavior, a fairly high amount given all of the other factors that we know can contribute to a child's risk of becoming violent. In contrast, lifetime or past exposure to violence accounted for just an additional 1 percent of the prediction of violent behavior once all of the other factors, including recent violence exposure, were taken into account. We have found the same pattern of influence for older adolescents as we did for young children, favoring the strong influence of recent exposure to violence compared to lifetime violence exposure.

The Case of School Failure

School failure plays an important role in determining a child's mental health and risk for engaging in aggressive, delinquent, or violent behavior. It is, fortunately, a phenomenon that we can do something about, compared to changing a child's personality or genetic makeup, so its role in violence and mental health deserves some special mention. When school failure is present, it tends to be associated with other negative outcomes such as disruptive and delinquent behavior, which is a common co-occurring problem. The association between academic failure and delinquency or antisocial behavior is clear even very early in elementary school, and behavior and academic problems in elementary school often preclude high school dropout and academic failure. Most adolescents don't just decide one day to drop out of high school. Rather, they have been experiencing academic and behavior problems for a long time before they actually drop out.

In a recent study that tracked children over many years, 45 percent of the delinquent youth were delayed in reading, and 36 percent were delayed in writing by the second grade. By junior high school, 50 percent of the delinquent youth were delayed in all academic areas, compared to approximately 18 percent of nondelinquent youth.[8] Another study of over 2,000 fourteen-year-old delinquent youth found that in the eighth grade most had academic achievement scores across subjects at the third- and fourth-grade levels.[9]

Studies that track children over many years have also shown that academic achievement and delinquency are strongly linked, because as one increases, the other seems to decrease, and vice versa. This is not a recent phenomenon but one that has held since research on delinquency in the early 1900s. Reviews of the major studies in the field show that poor academic performance predicts delinquency, even after taking into account the impact of poverty. Even students who have a history of offending or delinquent behavior engage in less problem behavior once they begin doing better in school. The longer a child remains out of school, however, the less likely he is to return, and the more likely the cycle of delinquent behavior and academic failure is to be reinforced and perpetuated over time.

One common theme across several theories of the development of delinquency and violence focuses on the fact that delinquent youth generally experience problems processing information, and in particular that they have problems with reading and math. Children with cognitive deficits or problems with attention will have more trouble with learning and will be more frustrated at school, making school a pretty unpleasant place to spend one's time. If a child becomes frustrated, he will often act out and become a behavior problem. This continues to affect his own academic achievement (you can't learn the material if you're not paying attention in class), but it also disrupts the ability of other students in the class to learn and takes up the teacher's time (because he has to stop what he's doing to discipline the child in order to maintain some order in the classroom). When this occurs, the likelihood that a student will be disciplined or suspended increases, and once a student is suspended, the chance that he will stay out of school increases significantly.

Chronic school absence and truancy are well-known predictors of academic problems, school failure, and delinquency.[10] We can usually pick up a trend by about the fifth or sixth grade. If a student is always absent or cutting school by the sixth grade, he is going to have a very hard time succeeding in middle school and making the transition to high school. Several studies, for example, have linked fifth-grade attendance rates with the likelihood of dropping out of high school.

The overall dropout rate during the past decade has been reported as approximately 11 percent.[11] Students typically drop out of school for three reasons: (1) school-based reasons (e.g., lack of attachment to school, they find school boring, they are truant, they don't get along with teachers, or they have negative experiences at school); (2) wanting or needing to find a job; and (3) personal reasons (e.g., not getting along with parents, being expelled from home, friends dropping out, getting pregnant, or using/abusing drugs or alcohol). Most of the reasons for dropping out of school are also associated with mental health problems and an increased risk for violence.

School staff perceptions of a student also have been found to play a role in academic achievement and misbehavior. Students who are perceived by teachers or staff to be at risk of engaging in antisocial or delinquent behavior are more likely to be punished, excluded, and controlled than to have their problems addressed appropriately by the school. The lack of appropriate intervention at school can further perpetuate the likelihood of academic failure because over time students viewed as troublemakers are not typically provided with many opportunities to succeed. By using aversive consequences, school officials may be increasing student apathy toward school and academics generally.[12]

CHAPTER FOUR

IT ALL BEGINS WITH FAMILY: SOCIALIZATION, VIOLENCE, AND MENTAL HEALTH

Just about every morning, Katie and I sit down and share a bowl of Wheaties or some yogurt. As soon as I pour cereal and milk into a bowl, she walks over to me, leans against my leg, opens her mouth, and says, "Eat." I'm not sure if she really likes the taste of the cereal or if she really just likes the interaction that I have with just her (and not her brothers and sister) early in the morning. What really sticks with me is how animated and happy she is when I tip a spoonful into her mouth, with milk inevitably dripping down her chin. She smiles, she sways back and forth, sometimes kicking one leg up in the air, spins around, and then comes back over to me, mouth open, saying, "more." Sometimes she climbs up onto the couch next to me and holds on to my arm as I spoon cereal into her mouth. She acts disappointed when I am finally left to exclaim, "all gone!" She's like a little bird waiting for its mother to put the worm in her mouth, craning her neck, looking upward into my eyes in anticipation.

All children form an attachment to their parents. It's practically inevitable. It's certainly normal. Sometimes the bond doesn't form very quickly. Sometimes it doesn't seem like it forms at all, as in the case of a child with autism. Sometimes the "fit" between mother and child isn't quite right. Maybe the infant or toddler is particularly hard to settle down and is easily irritable or colicky, and the mom has a low tolerance for crying. Sometimes, in extreme circumstances of abuse or neglect, the attachment between caregiver and child is formed for all the wrong reasons, like fear or anxiety.

In whatever shape or form the attachment between a child and care-giver occurs, it is clear that parents have a significant influence over their child from the earliest days of that child's very existence. A mother's influence begins in utero, where what she does while pregnant and how she treats her body will affect her developing child. The attachment begins in infancy, with mother-infant communication almost hardwired biologically. Infants first focus on the mother's eyes as a way of perceiving their environment, before they focus on other things going on in the world around them. Mothers naturally hold infants in their arms at just the right distance so their children can clearly focus on their faces. Mothers can differentiate the subtle differences in types of crying from their children, those that mean they are hungry from those that mean they are upset or scared.

Attachment between a parent and a child affects development throughout the child's lifetime. A warm, safe, and secure sense of attachment can lead to a child's developing a healthy identity, a sense of self-confidence, an ability to regulate emotions, and a belief that his own actions will produce consequences as opposed to feeling like things mostly happen out of chance or luck. When an unhealthy attachment forms, children grow up being more anxious and insecure. They seem to struggle more in their search for a healthy sense of purpose and direction, and they have more problems developing mature relationships with others.

Early animal studies and work with orphans told us a great deal about the importance of attachment. Years ago a researcher by the name of Harlow studied rhesus monkeys, curious about the ways mother and infant monkeys formed their relationships, particularly with respect to how infants depended on their mothers for survival. For many years up until that point (the 1940s), social scientists and pediatricians believed that early in the mother-infant relationship, what was most important was for parents to provide for their infant's basic needs—food, clothing, shelter, and warmth. There was little attention paid to any other relationship issues. Infants couldn't talk, had undeveloped brains, and could barely move about, so why would anyone expect they would play any role in actively forming a relationship with anyone? Harlow thought there was more to the mother-infant relationship than providing basic needs, so he devised a clever experiment to find out.

Harlow set up a cage so that it contained two fake rhesus monkeys, symbols of surrogate mothers. One monkey was made of wire mesh and held a bottle full of food. The other monkey was covered in soft, fuzzy cloth, but had no food. Harlow took a group of infant monkeys and deprived them of food and nourishment for several days. Once the infant monkeys became desperate with hunger, he released them into the cage of the two fake monkeys. The infant monkeys could go one of two ways— they could go into the section of the cage with the wire mesh monkey and eat, or they could go into the cage with the soft, furry monkey where there was no food. Harlow found that infant monkeys, even when they were suffering from starvation and were near death, preferred to go into the cage with the cloth monkey rather than go to the wire mesh monkey and food. Infants preferred the warmth and ability to hug and cuddle more than they needed the food.

Early experiences with children in Russian orphanages also told us some things about the importance of interacting with infants in a meaningful way. As noted above, for years the thinking was that it was mainly important to meet an infant's basic needs. So, infant orphans in the Soviet Union were housed in large warehouselike facilities with a few caregivers providing for many, many children at one time. Pictures show cribs lined up and down rows, with one or two adults milling around, available to change diapers or provide a bottle of milk when an infant cried. To simplify the story a little, one day a nurse brought in some toys for one of the infants to play with in her crib. The nurses immediately began to notice that the child became much more animated in her crib, moved around more, and began babbling more than children who did not have toys in their cribs. It turns out that toys provided a degree of stimulation for the infants that they didn't have before. Soon, nurses were providing colorful toys for all of the infants in their care, and they found that children interacted much more with their environment when adults did things to stimulate them beyond the mere providing of basic needs. This whole awareness of development in infancy has lead to our increased appreciation for the importance of infant-caregiver (parent) attachment and to a whole movement toward stimulating toys, reading to infants, an appreciation for the socialization they receive in day care settings, and a recognition that brain development is significantly impacted by early interactions, environmental stimulation, and the quality of a child's relationships with significant others.

What do these experiences from years ago tell us? Socialization begins at home, from the earliest moments of an infant's interactions with adults.

While much is present genetically and biologically at birth, future development, how those genes and that biological predisposition are expressed, depends on socialization experiences and environment.

There are many factors that can interfere with the development of secure attachment, and many of these same factors are related to the development of later behavior problems. For example, life stress can cause problems with the formation of a healthy attachment between parent and child. A depressed mother may have a hard time expressing warmth and nurturance toward her child, especially if the child has a difficult temperament. Parents in homes where financial stress is high or where marital conflict or violence is common also have children with poor attachment. Parents who utilize inappropriate or ineffective parenting strategies are also more likely to have children who grow up to become aggressive or violent.

Of course, not all children grow up to become violent. Most estimates are that only about 3 to 5 percent of all children grow up to become violent adolescents or adults, those who engage in violence to intentionally hurt others, who continue to prey on others until they are forced to stop via incarceration or death. Another 3 to 5 percent of individuals may engage in opportunistic violence or violent behavior that is not directed toward another person (e.g., criminal vandalism), but these outcomes are still the exceptions rather than the rule.

The Coercive Cycle of Parent-Child Interactions

One intriguing phenomenon related to the risk for future delinquent and antisocial behavior is a parenting style that can be described as coercive parent-child interactions.[1] Just about every town these days has large discount stores that sell goods on a reduced basis, especially things like paper products, toys, and soda pop. We have one close to where we live, and I frequent it often, especially when we are in need of diapers or wipes. I am the anointed discount store shopper in my family, as my wife refuses to go to this particular store. I'm not sure if it is the aggressive drivers in the parking lot always trying to get the closest space, the cluttered merchandise in the aisles, or the fact that it always takes at least twenty minutes in line to purchase your goods no matter how many people are in line or how much stuff you have to buy. Whatever the specific reason, my wife is resolute in her refusal to shop there (but that's probably a different chapter altogether).

One day a few years ago, I headed to the discount store to buy diapers for Ellen, who was about two years old at the time. I brought along Joseph, who was probably six or so, and Patrick, who was four. I like to bring them along to get them out of the house, and of course to teach them early in life about how much things cost in a store, that money doesn't grow on trees, and that, when necessary, I also walked several miles in deep snow to school or to the store to purchase the last can of SPAM or the last box of powdered milk (remember, I came from a family of eight children, so that is actually true). Anyway, I drove to this store and parked several rows away from the entrance to avoid the mad rush of cars for the closest parking spaces. Of course, this presents a different challenge, one of tightly gripping your child's hand and racing through the parking lot fast enough to avoid one of those cars screeching into an open spot. I once thought of making them wear orange hunting vests and hats when we went shopping so they would be more easily seen by drivers, but I thought better of it when we ran into some of their friends one day at the mall.

So, gripping Joe in one hand and Patrick in the other, we bound through the parking lot and jumped up onto the curb. As we walked toward the store entrance, I dutifully announced to no one, "Boys, now listen up," to which Joseph curtly replied, "Yeah Dad, we know."

"Know what?" I asked curiously. "How do you know what I'm about to say?"

"You're going to tell us that we aren't here to buy any toys today, Dad, OK? We get it," Joe sighed. Patrick just rolled his eyes. Well, Joseph was right on the money, so to speak.

"Yep, that's right," I replied, proud that Joseph was actually thinking like a rational, reasonable adult (even though he was only six).

As soon as we entered the front door of the store, I announced, "Let's go get the diapers. Dinner is waiting." (Remember, it takes twenty minutes in line, no matter what.) Anxious Joe, as expected, kept right in step as I strode down the first aisle, heading toward the diapers. Patrick, on the other hand, stopped right next to the vegetables and asked, "Dad, can we just go *look* at the toys? I know we can't buy anything today. I just want to *look*. Please!"

Well, I thought, what a nice way to ask, and he even said he recognized the limits that I so thoughtfully had placed on him *before* we went into the store. I looked quickly over at Joe, and he had that pleading look in his eyes, with his hands joined in prayer. So I relented, but only briefly: "OK, we'll go over to the toy aisle for *two* minutes!" We marched over to the toys. The boys scurried down the aisle. I stood at the end of the aisle, leaning against the display of peanut-butter crackers, looking at my watch.

"One more minute," I declared. Patrick looked up and then quickly called out, "Dad, I can't reach the toy soldiers, can you get them down for me?" You know the ones. These were the little green ones that you used to set up in your family room and shoot over with rubber bands. With my brother, you tried to get the really thick rubber bands, because you could sometimes take out more than one at a time. The lying down guys were the best ones to get on your side, because the rule was you actually had to flip them over for them to be considered dead, and that was hard to do with a regular red rubber band.

"Patrick, you know we're not here to buy toys today," I said, reminding him of my earlier (but not too much earlier) request.

"Yeah dad, I know. I just want to touch 'em," he quickly replied.

So I got the soldiers down and handed them to Patrick, and he immediately began to fondle the bag with great affection, and his eyes began to gleam over. "Thirty seconds!" I announced, because you're always supposed to give your kids warnings to prepare them for transitions, especially in public places, right?

"Time's up. Let's go." I turned and began walking away. Joseph, again, was right on my heels. I got past the pharmacy and crossed the cereal aisle, only two away from the diaper aisle, and something didn't feel right. I stopped and turned around. There was Joe, practically tripping over my heels when I stopped. "Joe, where's Pat?" I said with worry in my voice.

"I don't know, Dad! Maybe he's lost," Joe said anxiously.

"Let's retrace our steps," I replied, sure that I would soon hear on the store's public address system, "Will the parent of Patrick please come to the customer service desk?" We walked back to the toy aisle, and as I turned the corner of the aisle and looked down, there was Patrick sitting on the floor. Not only was the bag of army guys sitting there between his legs, but he was now surrounded by several other toys, most of which I couldn't make out from a distance, but a few made noises that I was sure I didn't want in my house.

Still standing at the end of the aisle, I called, "Patrick, let's go!" About ten steps later, the feeling of not being complete came over me yet again. I turned, and still there was no Patrick. Returning to the end of the aisle, I looked down toward Patrick, and to be sure he heard me, my voice was a bit louder: "What are you *doing*?" Patrick looked up at me and exclaimed with near enthusiasm, but clearly laced with defiance, self-confidence, and a little bit of agitation, "Dad, I want a toy!"

"Patrick, you are not getting a toy," I said sternly. "I told you that before we came into the store, and you said OK." Patrick wouldn't give up. He got louder and he kicked, and soon toys began flying off the shelf. Patrick was on the ground, flailing around like a caught fish, yelling for anyone to hear, "I want a toy! I want a toy! I'm going to get a toy!" The army guys were jettisoned down the aisle. The sidewalk chalk top came off, and the chalk began rolling away. The Barbie was kicked over next to the G.I. Joe. This was not going well. It seemed like everyone in the store was now staring at us, staring at me. I felt embarrassed and even felt that somehow Patrick had set me up to look and sound like an impatient father.

I was angry and frustrated, and I was getting desperate. I bent over Patrick and spoke directly into his ear, only loud enough for him to hear me: "Patrick, if you don't stop right now and put those toys back, I will *never* bring you to this store again, and you will *never* get another toy for as long as I live!" Uh oh, I soon thought, what had I done? To cope with this nasty situation I had used the mother load of all threats! "No toys forever!" How in the heck was I going to back that up? How could I be so dumb?

I practically ran to the diaper aisle, Joe close behind. I grabbed the diapers off the shelf and marched to the closest checkout lane. Joseph tried to plead or mutter something as I walked, but I don't remember what he said. We got in line. We were four people back (of course), and even though we were in the express lane, it was taking a while for us to pay for the diapers.

"Joe, where's Pat?" I turned to ask. Just then, Patrick sauntered up to us in line, as if he had not a care in the whole world. He looked a little too smug for his own good, given what had just transpired in aisle three.

"Patrick, what is that you have under your arm?" I asked. And then it happened. So smooth, so self-assuredly that I almost couldn't believe I was seeing what I was seeing, Patrick pulled out the bag of army guys and tossed them into the basket, up until now holding only one jumbo packet of Ultratrim diapers. "You've got to be kidding me," I said to no one in particular. I looked around quickly, hoping for an out. The line was hopelessly packed. My mind began racing. "He's only four," I thought. "I can't send him back to return the army guys alone. Joe isn't old enough to take him either. I'm trapped. What to do?" Patrick remained defiant and exclaimed, "I want the army guys or I'm not ever going to do what you tell me to in a store ever again!" I quickly made the ultimate choice, the only clear alternative, the only outcome that could solve my dilemma. I gave in and bought Patrick the bag of army guys.

Oh boy. Who won? Patrick obviously won because I bought him the bag of army guys. The store won, because they got the purchase. What did Joseph learn? He just watched his brother get what he wanted by escalating his inappropriate behavior in a public place until it got to the point where I would give in. So, Joseph learned that maybe if he does the same thing in the same situation, he might also get what he wants next time.

Who else wins in this situation? The parent wins. By giving in to Patrick's demand for a toy, I stopped the very unpleasant, embarrassing tantrum in a public place. This is a form of negative reinforcement; we remove a negative consequence to reinforce something positive. By giving in to Patrick, I removed the negative feelings I was experiencing because of his tantrum, and something positive happened for me: I felt better because the frustration, anxiety, and embarrassment went away.

We can clearly see how this coercive parent-child-interaction cycle influences child behavior and reinforces their oppositional, defiant behavior. Our kids learn that if they manipulate us in the right way and push the limits on a situation just enough, they can get their way. Sometimes it happens because we don't want to be embarrassed. Sometimes it happens because we are too tired or just don't want to deal with the situation (remember, if there is no sound of breaking glass or blood-curdling screams coming out of the basement, everything must be OK, right?). In any event, we rarely think about this coercive interaction as something that is reinforcing to the parent. Sometimes it feels a lot better to get rid of the aversive, manipulative child behavior by giving in, because it is so very hard to stay consistent and follow through with consequences, especially if the consequences don't really fit the crime.

Parenting, and how we interact with our children, sets the stage for much of their socialization and learning, how they interact with others, how they handle opportunities to engage in misbehavior, how they approach a problem and try to solve it (or not), whether they put forth effort when faced with a difficult task or give up easily, whether they take responsibility for their own behavior or constantly seek ways to deflect blame, and how they form relationships with others.

Send in the Reinforcements

One way children learn from and are socialized by their parents is through the use of reinforcement of behavior, both desirable and inappropriate behavior. In general, we learn to do things and act in certain ways because we are positively reinforced for doing them. For example, when a child behaves in a prosocial way (e.g., trying to share a toy with another child), he will be more likely to do it again in the future if an adult lavishes him with smiles, positive voice tone, and verbal praise ("Good job, Katie! How nice of you to share your toys!"). This is positive reinforcement. There are other ways to increase the probability that a desired behavior will occur again in the future (e.g., allowance or money). The opposite of positive reinforcement is punishment. In its basic form, punishment is the application of something negative that is meant to reduce the likelihood that the target behavior will occur again in the future. An example of punishment would be yelling at your child when he has acted inappropriately. You hope the yelling will be a negative, undesirable experience for your child and will reduce the chances that the inappropriate behavior will occur again in the future.

There are many variations on positive reinforcement and punishment that we use to shape behavior. The third basic type of reinforcement is referred to as time-out, which involves removing something positive in order to decrease the occurrence of an undesirable or negative behavior. This occurs when an adolescent child comes home late, well after curfew, perhaps smelling of having partaken of cooling but potent beverages, and Mom or Dad exclaims, "You're grounded. Go to your room!" This is a form of time-out, removing your child from interaction with peers and the world in general (which interaction we assume is reinforcing for them) as a form of punishment to decrease the chance that they will come home late the next time. Of course, sending a child to his or her room is not what it used to be, so you have to be careful. It used to be that bedrooms were dark, lonely places where a child could be sent to dwell in solitude and prayer for hours on end without interruption, social interaction, or any other stimulation from the outside world (this was a little difficult if multiple siblings shared the same bedroom and were grounded at the same time, which made the bathroom come in handy. This was true until my older brother Jim flooded the bathroom during one particularly adventurous grounding).

These days, however, many children's bedrooms are solitary kingdoms. By that I mean that more children have their own bedrooms these days, whether this is because we live in bigger houses now than we used to growing up or we just have fewer kids than our parents did but live in the same size houses. It may also be that we have converted every possible square inch of our houses into functional living spaces so our children have the finished attic or basement as a bedroom. If a child's bedroom contains a television, DVD or VCR player, his own phone, his own computer hooked up to the Internet, and access to every other gadget you can think of, time-out to the bedroom is not exactly removing a child from things that are reinforcing. In fact, some children may begin to act out purposely so they can be sent to their room. Maybe there they can play on the computer in solitude without interruption from pesky siblings and without being nagged by frustrated parents. So, be careful how you use time-out and what you choose to use as punishment.

One of the most misunderstood forms of behavior management is negative reinforcement. Because we call it negative reinforcement, our first impression is that it works like punishment, applying something negative to reduce inappropriate behavior. However, the key here is to focus on the fact that it is a form of reinforcement, which is always aimed at increasing a target behavior. So, negative reinforcement actually involves the removal of something negative in order to increase the likelihood of something desirable or positive. An example of negative reinforcement would be lifting a child's grounding because he has been so good since you imposed the punishment. The thinking is that by lifting the grounding (the punishment) you will reinforce the good behavior that your child is now showing you.

This was a favored strategy among my siblings. In short, it didn't really matter how long you were grounded for in the heat of the moment. This task was usually handled by my mother, as my father often traveled for work and was not at home in the early part of the evenings after school. Also, because there were eight of us, it was easy to take a snapshot of our house and find one of the kids engaged in some sort of inappropriate behavior or mischief. However, once the grounding was officially in place (which was still better than the wooden spoon), the contest among the kids was all about who could get out of the grounding the quickest. It was amazing how much homework got done, how often the garbage was taken out, and how many offers there were to change the baby's diaper or walk Crunchy, our German shepherd (even without being asked) during these competitive times of getting-out-of-grounding days. Table 4.1 summarizes the four main types of reinforcement and punishment strategies and whether they result in an increase ($\uparrow$) or decrease ($\downarrow$) in the target behavior.

Some examples may help illustrate the different kinds of reinforcement. A strategy that applies something positive (e.g., saying "good job" after your child puts the dishes away) is a form of positive reinforcement that is meant to increase the chances that your child will put the dishes away again in the future. Conversely, removing something positive is a form of time-out, which is meant to reduce or decrease the chance that your child will engage in the target behavior again in the future. If a child is clowning around in the classroom, for example, his teacher may expel him to a chair in the hallway. The teacher may notice that the attention he gets for clowning around (e.g., the other kids laugh at him) is positively reinforcing his inappropriate behavior. To stop it from continuing, the teacher removes the positive reinforcement (by sitting in the hallway, the child stops getting attention from his peers for clowning around), with the intent of decreasing the chance that the inappropriate behavior will continue.

Two other variations of reinforcement warrant mention here, as they impact how we interact with, discipline, and socialize our children on a daily basis. The first is extinction. This is one way to try to diminish or get

Table 4.1. Types of Reinforcement and Punishment

	Apply	Remove
Positive	Positive Reinforcement ($\uparrow$)	Time Out ($\downarrow$)
Negative	Punishment ($\downarrow$)	Negative Reinforcement ($\uparrow$)

rid of a behavior. It works like this. Let's say you want your child to learn a specific behavior. The quickest way to do this is to reinforce the behavior (or something close to it) every time it occurs. This is continuous reinforcement. So, if you want me to take out the garbage, the quickest way to get me to do it and keep doing it is to give me a quarter every time I take out the garbage, get close to the garbage can, ruffle the plastic bag, and so on. Once the desired behavior is established, however, it can be extinguished if you stop giving out quarters every time as a form of reinforcement. Without the expected reward, I would stop doing the behavior.

This also works for undesirable behaviors. Sometimes even negative attention can be reinforcing. While this doesn't make much intuitive sense, as parents we all know that sometimes our children act out to get our attention, even if it is negative. Being yelled at is better than being ignored. So we have to be careful that our attempts at what we think is punishment don't actually turn into a form of positive reinforcement for our children. Remember, it's about trying to understand a child's motivation for the behavior that is important, not our belief or perception of what motivates him to act the way he does. So, ignoring an inappropriate behavior can sometimes extinguish it (get rid of it), even though our natural reaction is to pay attention to it via yelling, talking about it with our child, grounding him, or threatening him. Most teachers have mastered the use of time-outs and of ignoring inappropriate behavior in their classrooms. If they haven't figured these skills out in the first few years of teaching, they're probably not teaching anymore.

The last variation on the reinforcement theme is how we vary the type and intensity of our reinforcement schedules in order to modify, change, or maintain certain behaviors. As noted above, the quickest way to get somebody to learn something new is to provide reinforcement every time the desired behavior occurs. Continuous reinforcement is also the easiest to extinguish because once we stop reinforcement, which is now expected every time, your child will quickly cease the desired behavior. How do we prevent this from happening? We're bound to run out of quarters, or at least we're bound to not be able to see the behavior every time it happens and be in a position to reinforce it. Even if we have an endless supply of quarters, our child will eventually tire of getting them or will want more than just one quarter, and we'll need to find something else or something more to motivate him to take out the garbage.

The way to get around this dilemma is to begin to vary the amount of reinforcement we give our children so they don't expect it every time they do something desirable or appropriate. This is also necessary because we want our children to develop a sense of efficacy or control over their own behavior, and we want them to internalize the behavior and do it because it is reinforcing to them (i.e., it feels good to help someone else), as opposed to only engaging in the behavior because they expect a reward or reinforcement for doing it. We want them to take out the garbage because they have responsibilities as a member of the family to contribute to the daily chores, not because they're going to get a reward every time. We can vary our types or schedules of reinforcement based on the number of responses or on the time interval between responses. Table 4.2 summarizes these types of reinforcement schedules.

If we vary the reinforcement we give out over a *fixed period of time*, we are spreading out the schedule and rate of reinforcement, so we are reducing the chance that the desired behavior will be extinguished. But, after a while, we'll see spikes in productivity immediately before and immediately after the reward, but a decline in performance at other times. A regular paycheck is a good example. There have been many studies that show increases in job productivity and satisfaction around payday, but lower levels of output at other times of the month. We can also dole out reinforcement based on a *fixed number of desired responses*. An example of this type of reinforcement is when we pay for a specific number of pieces assembled in a factory by a worker.

One way to handle the problem of fixed time and expectation of reinforcement is to vary when the reinforcement occurs over an *average number of times*. An example of this variable time schedule is the dividend payoff that holders of stock receive. They may receive dividends on stock holdings on average four times a year, but these may be awarded in month one, again in month three, but not again until months nine and twelve.

Table 4.2. Schedules of Reinforcement

Type of Reinforcement	Example
Fixed time	Paychecks every 2 weeks
Variable Time	Stock dividends
Fixed number	Piecemeal factory work
Variable number	Slot machines

You know you're going to get four payouts during the course of the year, but you just don't know when. The last type of variable reinforcement is that given out based on an *average number of responses* (as opposed to an average amount of time). The best example of this type of reinforcement is the schedule programmed into slot machines. The payouts are spread out across an average number of pulls of the lever, not a fixed number (e.g., every five pulls, there is a payout), and not an average passage of time (e.g., you get a big payoff every half hour you play the machine). You can win on a slot machine on consecutive pulls, or you can pull the lever a hundred times in a row and win nothing at all. Guess which type of reinforcement is the hardest to extinguish (i.e., produces the behavior hardest to stop).

What Did We Learn from the Salivating Dogs?

Animal studies have also told us a great deal about how the brain develops and responds to early trauma and stress. Many years ago, animals were used in experiments to learn about how we are conditioned to behave in different situations. The most famous of these studies were conducted by Ivan Pavlov. Using dogs in a laboratory setting, Pavlov showed how a natural stimulus (e.g., food) produces a natural response (e.g., salivation). For me, it's usually the presentation of peanut M&M's that produces the salivation. After observing this natural reaction to food, Pavlov began introducing the food while at the same time turning on a bright light. After a while, all Pavlov needed to do was turn on the bright light, and this would produce salivation in the dogs, even without the presentation of food. In other words, he produced a conditioned response (e.g., salivation) by presenting a stimulus in the environment that does not normally produce that response (e.g., a bright light). For those of you who have pets, you may get an excited reaction from your dog when you merely get the food dish out, before you actually present the dog with the food. Or your dog might jump up and down and bark at the mere sight of the leash, anticipating that you will take him out for a walk. These responses are conditioned similarly to the pairing of the light with the presentation of the food, so that eventually all you need is the light to produce the salivation, even in the absence of the food.

In the same way, we sometimes react to things in our environment that wouldn't normally produce that reaction; we've been conditioned to respond that way because our minds associate the stimulus with a specific response. This is one interpretation of how various memories and experiences can elicit PTSD-related behaviors and responses even if the memory or experience isn't normally associated with PTSD. Think of how hearing about a violent rape in the evening news can cause a woman to feel insecure, anxious, and unsafe because years ago she was also the victim of a violent rape. Just hearing about it on the news (i.e., the environmental stimulus) produces the memory and the conditioned response (anxiety, stress, and depression).

Can't We All Be Like Mike?

Beyond the use of basic types and schedules of reinforcements (and their many variations), and beyond being conditioned to respond to certain stimuli, children also learn how to behave through observation and modeling of others' behavior. This goes one step beyond the basic premise that we must be reinforced in one way or another to learn a new behavior. Most of us would agree that not all behavior is learned only after we are reinforced for it. We do many things (or don't do them) based on our anticipation of the consequences of the behavior, before we directly experience the reinforcement or punishment for engaging in the behavior for ourselves. For example, do we really need to go outside and get frostbite before we put gloves on to keep our hands warm? Most of us will put gloves on in anticipation that our hands will get cold if we don't. Our children learn these types of behaviors through various forms of modeling. We can tell them to put their gloves on and remind them why they put them on. We can remind them of how cold their hands are when they take their gloves off and play in the snow without them, and of how they would be warmer if they kept their gloves on. (Of course, this can also turn into rantings and ravings about the inevitability of frostbite and trips to the emergency room, where they will certainly have to take themselves because there is no way you are going to stop what you're doing to drive them there just because they chose to take their gloves off after you told them they needed to keep them on while they played outside in the snow!) These events serve as those teachable moments we've all heard about.

What makes an effective model? Children are more likely to model the behavior of someone they admire. Sometimes this is Mom or Dad or an older sibling. Sometimes it's a well-known actor or athlete like Michael Jordan. Remember how everyone used to exclaim how they wanted to be like Mike (the power of advertising at work)? Mr. Jordan also possessed some other characteristics of an effective model: he enjoyed high status and was rewarded in many positive ways for his behavior. Individuals are also more likely to model someone else's behavior (i.e., the modeling is more effective) if the model is more similar to the individual attempting to imitate the model. If you are an eight-year-old boy who is afraid of dogs, you are much more likely to be influenced by seeing another eight-year-old boy interact with a dog in a nonanxious, playful way than you would be to model the behavior of a forty-year-old woman, even if both scenarios depict someone interacting appropriately with a dog, with lots of positive reinforcement and reward. Finally, it is not enough just to have a model with high status who is rewarded for his behavior and who is similar to us. In the end, we have to have the skills and ability to successfully model the behavior. Alas, as much as many of us dreamed about being like Mike, none of us possessed the skill set (despite possessing the motivation) to be able to replicate his behavior on the basketball court.

Fortunately, most youth and even adolescents report that they most admire their parents, ascribe high status to them as role models, and share their values and general outlook on life. Thus, if we choose to, we as parents can be significant and effective role models for our children regarding a whole host of behaviors, attitudes, values, and belief systems. All we have to do is put forth a consistent effort to model the behavior we want our children to adopt as their own and then reinforce them in positive ways when they do so. This is easier said than done, but it is certainly not out of the realm of possibility, because we all have the ability to be good role models and parents to our children.

How to Be a Stylish Parent

Another aspect of parenting that is critical to long-term outcomes like aggression, antisocial behavior, academic achievement, and mental health has to do with the general style of parenting we use with our children. While there have been many studies of parents, most conceptualize parenting around four distinct styles that we tend to employ in our day-to-day interactions with our children. None of us uses any one style all the time, in all situations, or even with all of our children in the same way, but most of us probably fall into one or another category, generally speaking, and we know a lot about how our general approach to interacting with our children affects them emotionally, socially, behaviorally, and cognitively. What are these four styles?

In table 4.3, I've summarized each of the four major styles of parenting by labeling whether or not the style reflects a demanding or nondemanding style and whether the parent is generally supportive and available or more neglectful and unsupportive. The first style of parenting is the authoritarian style. The classic example of the authoritarian parent is the one who frequently exclaims to his children, "Just do it because I said so!" or "Don't ask me why; just do it!" This type of parent is highly demanding of his children but rarely offers support or any reason for what he demands.

At the other end of the parenting spectrum is the parent who makes very few demands of her child but who is very engaged and supporting. In some ways, this parent wants to be her child's best friend and believes that always being there to support and help him is far better in the long run than expecting him to do anything or to put forth any effort to accomplish tasks. This parent is likely to take stances such as, "It's OK, honey. You go out and play with your friends. No problem. You don't have to clean your room. I'll pick that stuff up for you." The permissive parent has few expectations of her children and makes few demands of them, but she is highly supportive and engaged, often to an extreme.

A rejecting or neglectful parent is neither demanding of his child nor available, emotionally or otherwise, to support his child. Did you ever, perhaps in a moment of anger or frustration, say to your child, "Just leave me alone. Get away from me. I don't want to be near you"? This is one example of rejecting your child. The ultimate form of long-term punishment and emotional neglect is to be a rejecting or neglecting parent. You basically just don't really care what happens to your children.

Table 4.3. Different Types of Parenting Styles

Type of Parenting	Way typically interact with children
Authoritarian	Demanding but unresponsive
Permissive (Laissez-Faire)	Not demanding but very responsive
Rejecting/Neglecting	Not demanding, not responsive, don't care
Authoritative	Demanding but responsive, supportive

A good friend of mine, who is now a highly respected community activist in the field of violence prevention, tells a compelling story of how he was rejected as a child by his mother and how, on the one hand, this rejection lead to his experiences with gangs in the infamous Cabrini Green housing complex in inner-city Chicago. On the other hand, he describes how her rejection probably saved his life. How can this be?

Bob (not his real name) was living in Cabrini Green with his mother, who had separated from Bob's father a few years earlier. He was ten. His mother suffered from some significant mental health issues (schizophrenia and depression) as well as from problems with substance use. Bob was not yet actively involved with any gang, and he would take purposeful routes home from school to avoid running into the older, gang-involved youth. One day he found himself on the wrong street, and he was cornered by several older youth who beat him in the head with a brick ten times, representing the ten bricks in the pyramid symbol of the Vice Lords gang. This beating was how gang members often initiated new members.

Bob ran home, bleeding from the head. As soon as he entered his apartment, he found himself standing on the newly installed white carpet. Instead of expressing concern for his condition or predicament, Bob's mother's only comment was, "Get off my new carpet before you get any blood on it!" Bob quickly made his way out into the hallway, where he was met by the older youth who had beaten him with the brick. The leader put his arm around Bob's shoulder and said, "See, man? She don't love you. You come and hang with us. We're your family now." Bob entered the Vice Lords gang at ten and lived on the streets for several more years, dropping out of school, selling drugs, and always carrying a firearm.

One day a couple of years later, Bob was standing on a street corner with his best friend. He was now "mature" beyond his twelve years of age. A car sped by. Shots rang out. Bob didn't react quickly enough to dive out of the way, but he didn't have to. His best friend jumped in front of him, was shot several times, and died later that day.

As tragic as that moment was for Bob, what happened after that changed his life. As he tells the story, a police officer who responded to the incident made a point of trying to find Bob's mother, who had had no contact with him since he left on that fateful day two years earlier. By this time, Bob had no idea where his mother lived. The police officer persisted. It took him several days to track Bob's mother down, but he finally did.

When the police officer finally got hold of Bob's mom, she rejected him one last time. "I don't want him," she told the officer. "I can't take care of him." The officer persisted. Was there anyone else who could take Bob in? Any other relatives in Chicago? No, but he had grandparents who lived in Alabama. With few other options, the police officer put him on a Greyhound bus to Alabama, where he went to live with his grandparents.

Bob credits the interest the police officer took in him with turning his life around. He went on to complete high school and college, where he excelled in athletics. He served time in the military after college and is now a respected community activist. He turned out to be one of the resilient ones, but he wouldn't have been able to do it without the support of that one committed adult, the police officer who persisted and followed through and got him on that bus to Alabama. Of course, we can't forget the tremendous commitment and support he received from his grandparents, who took him in and helped raise him despite great sacrifice on their part.

The last type of parenting style is the authoritative style. The authoritative parent has high expectations of her children and often makes demands of them, but she does so with significant support and encouragement. She is always available to her children for help if they need it, but not at the expense of relieving them of their own responsibilities. Children of authoritative parents do much better overall than do children of parents who primarily rely on the other forms of parenting. Children of authoritative parents do better in school academically by staying in school longer and achieving at higher levels than other children. They are much less likely to get into trouble as adolescents. They tend to make better choices when faced with problem situations, and they are much more likely to develop a sense of efficacy about their behavior—they know that what they do has outcomes they are responsible for, good and bad. They tend to work harder toward goals instead of expecting things to happen for them. They have higher self-esteem and more positive self-concepts than do other children.

The authoritative parenting style, demanding but responsive, has the most positive impact on adolescent outcomes. Parents are warm and nurturing, but they also have high expectations for their children and set realistic limits with consequences for misbehavior. Diana Baumrind, one of the leading researchers on parenting styles, found that authoritative parents tend to have children who are more academically and socially competent than do parents who utilize more authoritarian, neglectful, or permissive styles. Specifically, in a study of about 10,000 ninth- through twelfth-grade students, adolescents who characterized their parents as authoritative reported higher levels of academic achievement and competence, significantly lower levels of problem behavior, and significantly higher levels of psychosocial development than did adolescents from authoritarian, indulgent (i.e., permissive), or neglectful households.[2]

Compared to children with authoritative parents, those who grow up in homes where parents depend on a neglecting or rejecting style tend to do worse over time. They are more likely to drop out of school, to engage in delinquent or criminal activity as adolescents and young adults, and to eventually be involved in substance use. When they are older, they tend to get lower-paying jobs (partly as a function of their lower educational attainment), and they tend to experience more problems in their relationships.

At the extremes, parent-child relationships can be characterized by parents being overly strict and not allowing the child to think for him- or herself, or by parents being too permissive and neglectful, in effect allowing the child to act without consequence and without much monitoring. Parenting at either extreme, either too permissively or too strictly, appears to negatively affect adolescent behavior and academic performance. These negative effects include increased problem behaviors, a lower grade-point average, and a less positive orientation toward school. The frequent use of harsh and coercive discipline (as may be characteristic of authoritarian parents) can also contribute to a youth's aggressive and antisocial behavior, placing a child at increased risk for academic failure.

Parental Monitoring: Do You Know Where Your Kids Are?

Recently, parental monitoring has received a great deal of attention as a significant factor related to child outcomes and functioning, particularly as children mature through middle school and adolescence. Monitoring your child's whereabouts essentially involves knowing where your child is, what he is doing, and with whom. In practical terms, it may involve having clear expectations for where children are allowed to go, who they are allowed to hang out with, and at what time they need to be home at night. Is your child expected to call home if he is going somewhere other than where you expect him to be? Does he call home if he is going to be late? Are there clear consequences for violating family rules with respect to curfew and activities with peers? Parental monitoring, and how effectively and consistently we do it with our children, has been the topic of research and discussion involving child academic achievement, delinquent behavior, substance use, and exposure to and victimization from violence. With respect to delinquency, for example, we know that how effectively parents monitor their children (by child report) is related to whether or not a child is engaged in chronic delinquency or just occasionally gets into trouble. The more thoroughly children are monitored, the less frequent is their delinquent behavior. Lack of parental monitoring has also been linked to how likely it is that an adolescent will get into fights and have lower academic achievement.

Most parents are well aware of the challenges associated with the hours between 3 and 6 p.m., most often described as after-school time. This is the period of the day when child and adolescent victimization from violence is highest. Nearly one-fourth of youth crime happens between 2 and 6 p.m. on school days. One in five violent crimes (e.g., sexual assault, robbery, aggravated assault) among juveniles occur during after-school hours, and the frequency of violent crime is about four times greater in the after-school period than during curfew hours. This is the period of the day when most unsupervised adolescent activity occurs, including sexual activity and substance use. Historically, there has been much concern about latchkey children, those who come home from school and spend several hours on their own, without adult supervision. While it is hard to determine exactly the number of children regularly left unsupervised after school, studies from ten years ago suggest that at least two million children under the age of thirteen care for themselves, and these numbers are undoubtedly higher today. The assumption has been that these youth are at high risk for engaging in delinquent behavior, experimenting with substances, participating in sexual activity, and generally getting into trouble with their peers.

In the early 1990s, I conducted a study of just over 1,100 middle school students in a large southwestern city. These students were in the sixth and seventh grades, so they were mostly eleven and twelve years old,

not nearly as old as youth in studies that survey adolescent problem behaviors like substance use and delinquency. The question we posed
(among others) was simply, "What do you most often do after school?"
The responses were then collapsed into one of five groups: (1) home with
parent or other adult (the largest group, over four hundred youth), consisting of all adolescents who said they typically went home to be with an
adult or to a friend's house where a parent or other adult was present; (2)
home alone, for students who went home where no peers, siblings, parents, or other adults were present; (3) home with sibling but no adult present; (4) took part in a school activity (youth regularly participated in some
organized activity like sports or clubs); and (5) being with a friend, no
adult present, consisting of those who reported going home with a friend,
to a friend's house, being with a friend in general, or going to the mall, all
with no adult present. Remember, this study was conducted in the early
1990s, well before we became much concerned about latchkey children or
the time children spent at shopping malls with their friends. This was also
before the age of pagers and cell phones, which have recently taken the
place of parents as the monitoring agents of their children's whereabouts.[3]

So, what did we find? We expected that children home alone, without
an adult present, the so-called latchkey kids, would report the highest levels of problem behavior given that they consistently experienced the lowest levels of parental monitoring and adult supervision during these
high-risk after-school hours. Contrary to our expectations, though, across
every outcome we assessed, adolescents at home with a sibling and no
adult present and adolescents with a friend and no adult present reported
higher levels of problem behavior compared to youth at home after school
with an adult present. In addition, youth who were home alone were not
significantly different than those at home with an adult present on any
outcome measure, including substance use. This study of middle school
students, which is consistent with the findings of more recent studies of
adolescents, highlights the role of peers and parents as important risk and
protective influences on early adolescent behavior and well-being.

In addition to the findings for overall risk of delinquent behavior and
substance use, we have also shown that for early and middle adolescents,
a lack of parental monitoring is associated with an increased susceptibility
to pressure from peers to engage in inappropriate behavior. For many adolescents, even if they are not normally predisposed to act out in a negative

way, they will participate when given the *opportunity* to engage in problem behavior, particularly in the presence of their friends. The pressure to be popular and feel like one belongs to a group can, at times, outweigh the pressure an adolescent feels to do the right thing. In middle school, for example, being popular is the number-one priority among young people, far ahead of earning good grades or getting along well with parents.

IT HAPPENS EVERY DAY IN EVERY WAY: CHILDREN EXPOSED TO VIOLENCE

One day several years ago, my wife and I went shopping late at night at a large discount store. It was the holiday season, and we had to pick up some last-minute gifts for the kids. While we were walking back to our car in the parking lot, we noticed that a woman had pulled quickly into the parking lot and was speeding down the aisle where we were walking. I turned to say something to my wife like, "Watch out! I can't believe she's driving so fast," but as soon as I turned toward her, a pickup truck came barreling into the lot close behind the first car, wheels screeching. The woman in the first car stopped her car right next to us. The pickup truck pulled up right to the back of her car and bumped it. A large man jumped out of the cab of the truck and ran up to the car, kicking it with his feet and pounding on the hood and the windows. He was yelling at the woman, something about cutting him off in traffic. My wife and I stopped cold in our tracks. My wife turned to me and said something like, "He can't do that to that poor woman." She turned and began to walk toward the car. By this time, a small crowd had gathered.

It was clear that my wife was going to try to intervene. The only problem was that she was carrying our infant son in her arms, and I was not about to let her get into the middle of an escalating conflict. I grabbed her by the arm and said, "No, let *me* go," and I quickly made my way toward the altercation. In the meantime, the man had gone back to his truck and had pulled something out that looked like a baseball bat. He began swinging at the back of the car. Understandably, the woman in the car was frantic. No one else was doing anything but watching what was unfolding. I quickly moved behind the man with the bat. "Hey, calm down, pal," was all I got out of my mouth before the man swung his arm around and hit me in the side of the face. I went down hard. I think hitting me caught him off guard, as he seemed jolted back to the present, out of his state of rage. He stopped. "Oh man, I didn't know you were there," he said. By this time, someone from the store came out, and several other people came over as a police car came into the parking lot.

Fortunately, I wasn't really hurt, but as I got up I noticed that there was a woman and several children in the pickup truck. The woman in the car also had a couple of kids in the backseat. I couldn't help wondering what all those kids must have been thinking given what they had just witnessed. The other thing I remember is being upset that so many people basically stood by and watched this incident unfold without trying to intervene before the conflict escalated to violence.

Children are exposed to a great deal of violence at home, in their neighborhoods, at school, and in the media. I talk specifically about school and media in other chapters, and we've already talked a bit about socialization at home, but I think it's important to get a sense of the violence that children are exposed to on a daily basis in their lives, and to understand the impact this can have on their development and socialization. Violence can affect children even if they are not chronically exposed to or victimized by abuse and neglect. This chapter also reviews some of what we have found over the last several years from a local initiative serving children and families exposed to domestic violence, aptly referred to as the Children Who Witness Violence Program.

How Much Violence Are Children Exposed To?

The major setting for violence in America is the home. Estimates suggest there are six million children abused or neglected each year in the United States. In countable, reported maltreatment cases, 25 of every 1,000 children are abused or neglected to such an extent that they come to the attention of authorities. In the United States alone, 40 percent of all murder victims under the age of eighteen are killed by a family member. Exposure to violence (being a witness to or being victimized by violence) is not confined to the home, however. Large community surveys of youth show that children are exposed to high levels of violence at home, in their neighborhood, and at school. In our own survey of over 3,700 adolescents in high school, nearly 40 percent of boys and 50 percent of girls reported that they saw someone else being slapped at home, and nearly 20 percent of adolescents reported witnessing a beating at home in the past year.[1]

Rates of *victimization* from violence at home were also high, with one in ten girls reporting they had been beaten at home, and on average about one in four adolescents reporting they were threatened by someone else at home. Nearly half of adolescents, boys and girls, reported that they had been hit at home, and significantly more girls than boys reported being the victim of sexual assault (which was not reported by setting) at some point in the past year. (See table 5.1.)

Rates of witnessing violence are generally higher than rates of actual victimization, and in our surveys of children, we have also found this to be so. What has been unsettling for us is the unusually high number of students who report witnessing violence in their daily lives, across settings. Even the youngest children are not immune to violence. As many as eight out of ten children report they have seen someone else threatened with violence at school or have seen someone else beaten up at school. Nearly half of youth attending central city schools in our survey reported they had seen someone else stabbed or attacked with a knife in the past year, and having a gun pointed at them was not such an unusual experience for any

Table 5.1. Percentage of Adolescents Victimized by Violence Within the Past Year

Type of Violence	Denver City (N=1,265)		Cleveland City (N=1,228)		Small Ohio City (N=862)		Cleveland Suburb (N=379)	
	Girls	Boys	Girls	Boys	Girls	Boys	Girls	Boys
Threatened at home	25.0	22.7	25.4	23.7	32.2	28.9	13.7	16.9
Threatened at school	38.6	42.4	30.5	34.8	38.9	48.3	12.1	32.3
Threatened in neighborhood	23.4	37.3	29.1	42.9	18.1	36.6	7.4	12.7
Hit/punched at home	44.1	31.9	47.4	36.1	56.2	39.8	34.2	26.5
Hit/punched at school	27.2	40.9	22.4	32.5	17.7	37.9	13.7	44.4
Hit/punched in neighborhood	9.0	24.2	17.6	31.6	11.1	23.7	2.6	12.7
Beaten at home	8.1	5.1	10.4	8.6	9.1	6.3	3.7	3.2
Beaten at school	5.2	10.4	3.6	9.1	4.0	5.6	.5	1.1
Beaten in neighborhood	5.2	10.5	8.8	22.4	4.0	11.5	5	3.2
Sexually abused/assaulted	16.2	4.6	16.3	7.0	17.3	3.9	12.1	1.6
Knife attack or stabbing	7.5	14.1	9.1	16.0	3.8	14.9	.0	5.8
Shot or shot at	11.9	28.3	10.1	33.4	4.0	18.8	.5	2.6

Table 5.2. Percentage of Elementary School Youth Witnessing Violence in the Past Year (grades 3–8)

Type of Violence	Central City (N=860)		Small City (N=837)		Rural (N=547)	
	Male	Female	Male	Female	Male	Female
Threatened at home	27.8	26.6	27.0	24.4	23.4	22.7
Threatened at school	72.9	68.7	81.0	80.2	68.3	64.8
Threatened in neighborhood	59.8	59.9	52.2	48.6	34.5	30.1
Slapped/hit/punched at home	45.6	50.4	37.2	41.8	37.1	38.0
Slapped/hit/punched at school	80.8	77.2	78.7	73.9	74.2	65.6
Slapped/hit/punched in neighborhood	68.1	70.1	57.9	51.9	36.1	35.3
Beaten up at home	33.8	34.5	19.4	21.4	16.6	15.6
Beaten up at school	78.0	75.7	67.9	67.5	62.2	55.1
Beaten up in neighborhood	70.2	72.3	48.6	43.2	33.8	29.4
Knife attack/stabbing	45.9	40.7	22.4	17.5	10.7	5.5
Gun pointed at you	51.4	42.1	24.9	15.8	20.0	9.4
Sexually abused	34.9	35.4	13.7	18.1	5.2	7.8

child, including those in rural settings. Table 5.2 summarizes data from our surveys with children in grades three through eight.[2]

Unfortunately, our data are consistent with other studies from around the country. In New Orleans, for example, 90 percent of school-aged children reported witnessing violence, with 70 percent of children reporting they had seen a weapon used and 40 percent saying they had seen a dead body.[3] In another survey of families referred to a pediatric outpatient clinic for services, one of every ten children under the age of six had witnessed a knifing or a shooting; nearly 20 percent had witnessed shoving, kicking or punching; and almost half had heard gunshots.[4] Our survey of elementary students in kindergarten through fifth grade in a southwestern city showed that for 17 percent of third graders, someone had tried to hurt them with a gun or knife in the past week, and nearly half of all third to fifth graders reported witnessing gang activity at school. A survey of first and second graders in Washington, D.C., found that 45 percent had witnessed a mugging, 30 percent had witnessed shootings, and 39 percent had seen dead bodies. In our assessments of children exposed to violence in northern Ohio (where the average age of respondents was six years old), nearly 10 percent report having seen a dead body in the past year, not including on television or in a funeral home.[5] More recent surveys of youth from the central city and from suburban and rural communities confirm these percentages and tell us that children and adolescents are being exposed to more frequent and more intense levels of violence. Today, the chance of being victimized by a violent crime at some point in your lifetime is greater than the chance of being injured in a traffic accident.

The Developmental Impact of Violence

Why should we be so concerned about the high rates of child exposure to violence, both witnessing and being victimized by violence? One concern is the significant effect that violence has on a child's mental health and well-being, a focus of this entire book. A related concern, however, is how violence can affect a child's overall development. This includes physical, emotional, social, and cognitive development.

Most parents significantly underestimate the level of distress their children may experience because of exposure to violence. This is particularly true for infants and toddlers. A common misconception is that very young children are relatively unaffected by violence because they are unable to process or understand what they see. They are also not able to tell us if they are afraid or hurt or depressed, nor can they very effectively draw pictures about their feelings. We've generally interpreted this perceived inability to express themselves as a barometer for their being relatively unaffected by violence. Over time we have come to understand that this is simply not the case.

Children are particularly vulnerable to violence because they have limited control over their context and setting. For example, young children have little control over with whom they live or where they live, so being exposed to violence in the home or neighborhood largely depends on adults who make those choices for them. A child does not choose to be born into a family where violent, aggressive behavior is a common occurrence, but if this happens, they have few options for removing themselves from that setting or for seeking help from outside sources. Think of how distressing it would be if the person you loved and depended on every day for support, affection, safety, and security was the same person who was beating you up, rejecting you, or being emotionally abusive to you, and you could do nothing to stop it.

A comprehensive review of the impact of violence on child development is beyond the purview of this chapter, but there are some excellent overviews of the significant developmental problems experienced by young people exposed to violence (see the appendix for available resources). While we know more about the effects of exposure to violence on adolescents, we are beginning to understand that infants and toddlers can also be significantly affected by violence, and not just if they are victims of serious abuse or neglect.[6] In many studies, young children exposed to violence seem to react in ways similar to children who have been victimized by abuse or neglect, particularly with respect to forming insecure attachments with caregivers and having difficulty developing a healthy sense of trust in their environments. Children who lack basic attachments and the ability to trust others will experience trouble later in life in their relationships, in school, and in their ability to become productive adults.

Violence also affects a child's ability to develop a sense of independence and the belief that they have some control over what happens to them. With young children, we sometimes refer to this as achieving mastery of their environment. It's like the infant in his crib who finally figures out that if he swings his fist in just the right way, he can make the colored ball move around in interesting ways. It's like the toddler who finally stacks three blocks in a tower and stands back, admiring her work, exclaiming, "I did it, Daddy! I did it!" These are important developmental milestones that contribute to a child's sense that she has some control over her environment, some ability to affect what is going on around her. Children exposed to violence are much more likely to be anxious and paranoid about their environment, not really knowing what to expect next. Or, if they are in an environment where violence and war are more chronic and common, they may develop a sense of learned helplessness about their situation, the converse of having a sense of mastery or control. What is learned helplessness? It is the sense that no matter what you try to do, you have no control over the outcome. It is observed in animal studies when a researcher places a rat in a tub of water and has it swim around and around trying to get out until it is utterly exhausted, finally realizing that no matter what it tries to do, it cannot escape from the water. Eventually, they give up and drown. Learned helplessness is significantly related to moodiness, depression, and self-control.

Children exposed to violence may experience high levels of anxiety or sleep disturbance, including nightmares. Studies have also shown that young children in violent environments have difficulty achieving bowel or bladder control and experience delays in language acquisition. All of these important developmental tasks involve a child's sense of initiative, autonomy, and whether he believes that with effort he can accomplish good things. Children exposed to violence also have difficulty in regulating their emotions. They are easily frustrated and tend to be impulsive in how they react to things. When they do react, it is more likely to be with anger and aggression than in a prosocial, competent way. When a child has trouble regulating his own emotions, he will also have trouble differentiating when others are angry, frustrated, happy, or depressed. When a child has difficulty reading the emotions of others, he is more likely to act and react in inappropriate ways to other people.

When we rob our children of their sense of control and accomplishment very early in life, we set them up for failure later on. They grow up believing that there is little hope for their future, and young people who lack any future orientation or hopefulness are much more likely to engage in aggressive, violent behavior. They exist in the here and now, have little concern over what happens to them or others, and feel no empathy. They don't believe they will live very long, and if they do, they see little joy in what awaits them. They trust no one, not even themselves. Their behavior is driven by a need for immediate gratification. They take no responsibility for their behavior or for the consequences of their actions. They feel like they have no support system, and their relationships with others are based on things and survival, not on warmth, affection, or secure attachment.

The Children Who Witness Violence Program

For the majority of young children, if they are exposed to violence, it will most likely occur in or near their home. Perpetrators of violence are most likely to be a parent, sibling, relative, or other adult caregiver. Remember, these are the same individuals with whom the young child is attempting to form secure attachments, the same individuals the child depends on for having her basic needs met, and the individuals who are the primary role models and socializing agents for the child.

Due to the high rates of child and adolescent exposure to violence and the mounting evidence of its significant impact on child and family well-being, a consortium of researchers, law-enforcement professionals, politicians, community leaders, and service providers came together in one metropolitan community to form and implement what has become known as the Children Who Witness Violence (CWWV) Program. The main goal of the program was to identify and intervene quickly with children who had witnessed a violent event and to provide crisis intervention services to those children and families. For families who agree and who need it, ongoing treatment is provided in the home by various community-based social service agencies.

While children are exposed to violence in a variety of settings, the consortium agreed that police officers frequently respond to incidents in which children have been exposed to violence at home, and that they (as opposed to teachers or emergency room nurses, for example) would be excellent first responders who could identify children and families in need of crisis intervention services. The program began with the participation of five separate communities in a large metropolitan area including two police districts in the largest urban city in the county. Initial referral criteria varied slightly between communities, but generally any child under the age of eighteen who witnessed violence, particularly an incident of domestic violence, was eligible for services.[7] For every child and parent who voluntarily agreed to receive services, a trained crisis intervention team visited with the family at least three times to provide help after the violent incident had occurred. For those who were willing (and only after the first visit was complete so that safety was assured and the initial crisis had passed), we asked a series of questions about what type of violence had occurred and about the child's mental health and behavior. For children older than eight, we asked them directly about their experience. For younger children, we asked parents or crisis intervention workers their observations about how the children were doing.

We began collecting information in 1999, and the program continues today. Over the first two years, we gathered information from over 3,000 children, the majority of whom (85 percent) had witnessed an incident of domestic violence, and also from youth who had witnessed homicides, suicides, and other violent events. What we have found reinforces the need to pay attention to the significant effect that violence has on the lives of young children.[8]

Descriptively, we were surprised by the persistently young age of children who were witnessing violence. Over 60 percent of youth who were exposed to domestic violence were under the age of ten, with an average

age of six years old. Three of four children directly witnessed the violent incident, and nearly one in ten were also directly victimized during the course of the event police responded to. In the majority of incidents (77 percent), a parent (usually the mother) was victimized, and another adult (usually the father) was the perpetrator (60 percent of the time). In nearly half of the cases, the victim suffered a visible injury as a result of the violence, and half of those were serious enough to require medical treatment. In a third of all cases, a weapon of some sort was used during the violent incident.

Even more troubling than the prevalence of domestic violence incidents and the number of children exposed to this violence on a regular basis was the effect that these incidents had on children. Nearly eight of ten children saw the violence as a direct threat to their safety or well-being, and nearly nine of ten viewed the event as a threat to others such as a younger sibling. Most children felt their parent had little or no control over the event's happening and could not prevent it from happening again, and they believed that another act of violence would probably occur again in the future. Most children were reported by their parents or by the crisis intervention worker to be experiencing clinically significant levels of anxiety, sleep disturbance, depression, and acting-out behavior. This means that symptoms were serious enough that they probably required immediate professional assessment and possible intervention.

What do these findings tell us about violence and mental health? Children are exposed to very high levels of violence in their homes, and they usually see the violence occur (as opposed to hearing about it or having it occur while they are asleep). Second, these incidents are more than just verbal shouting and often involve physical assault, the use of a weapon, and injury to the adult victim, the child witness, or the perpetrator. In many cases, a parent is arrested in front of the children after police arrive to intervene. Third, these incidents have a significant impact on child mental health and behavior, and the effects of this exposure do not go away overnight. We have found that children's emotional distress is high, and their feelings of helplessness and hopelessness about their situation are sometimes overwhelming to them. For the children and families that we have followed over time, we often see children having trouble in school with their behavior and their grades, and families continue to struggle through high levels of conflict and emotional upheaval. When children feel that their world is unpredictable, that violence can happen at any time (especially between people they love and depend on for their own safety and security), that it will probably happen again, and that they can do little to control it, they are at significant risk of experiencing long-term mental health and behavior problems. We place an extreme burden on these children, forcing them to find ways to cope with the everyday violence in their lives. Some children find ways to deal with it and function, but most children struggle to find the way to make things all right.

Media Violence and Child Mental Health

So, what's the big deal about violence in the media? It's been around forever. I remember being a regular watcher of *Combat* with Vic Morrow and Saturday-morning Roadrunner cartoons. While my siblings and I didn't have Internet access back then, and our only real video games were *Pong* and *Pacman*, we didn't grow up to be violent, so what's the big deal?

The big deal is that violence in the media has become more frequent, more intense, more easily accessible, and more real than violence in the media (and across mediums) used to be. When I was actively involved in seeing patients, I would regularly come into contact with parents who came to the clinic with highly anxious children. I remember one ten-year-old boy who presented with a generalized anxiety disorder. He was doing fine at school and was generally not very worried about what would happen to his mother while he was away attending classes during the day (a common worry among children with anxiety-related problems). After ruling out the most common sources of childhood anxiety, we got to discussing what he typically did during a day and when he felt the most anxious. "Well, when I wake up in the morning, we usually have the news on the television, and they always talk about somebody dying or getting hurt" was his general reply. How often does the news lead with a feel-good story about something positive? What percentage of the news is about something good happening in the world? This young man experienced a significant decrease in his feelings of anxiety as soon as his parents started more closely monitoring his television viewing, particularly limiting exposure to the morning and evening news.

What else has changed? Access. Children now have access to many more mediums for information than they have ever had before. Not only is the access broader, but it is more intense and immediate. News happens in other parts of the world, and children can learn about it minutes later. CNN is on the scene with live pictures of bombings, terrorist ambushes, and the effects of every natural disaster you can think of. When something dramatic or tragic occurs, you can't turn on a television or radio, log on to the Internet, or open a newspaper or magazine without seeing vivid images over and over again of what transpired. How many times did you see footage of the planes flying into the World Trade Center? How many pictures of the burning towers did you and your children see in the days, weeks, and months following 9-11? We are constantly bombarded with stories, images, and commentary about the worst things that happen in our world, not just in our neighborhoods, towns, or our own country.

I remember one particularly troublesome trend that occurred after the tragedy of the terrorist attacks on the World Trade Center. I have no doubt that someone at a local television station believed that what they were doing was positive and respectful, but I had to wonder about its potential impact on children. For weeks after 9-11, the station that broadcast the local major-league baseball team games had a permanent window displayed on the screen right next to the line for the game statistics. It was a simple "9-11-01" posted right next to the score, sometimes with a symbol of the American flag, sometimes with a picture of the World Trade Center, but it was always there. So, every time my children sat down to watch a baseball game, which was about every night, they were reminded, persistently, about what had happened. I was reminded, persistently, about what had happened. While this was meant to be a tribute to those who were killed that day, and the emphasis was on "we shall always remember, and never forget," one unintended consequence of that media strategy may have been a contribution to many viewers constantly reexperiencing the trauma of that event, brought on by the persistent images and reminders of that terrible day.

Media can play a powerful role in how it depicts violence and how this may impact viewers, including children, and there is sometimes a very fine line between one's responsibility to depict what is really happening in today's world, and understanding that when this is done without thought, critical discussion, and the depiction of the natural consequences of violence and disaster, the depiction of violence can have multiple negative effects, especially for the most vulnerable.

While being exposed to violence in the media will not make most of us go out and perpetrate violence, there is growing evidence of the generally negative impact of watching lots of violence in different mediums. There are four general effects on children that we should keep in mind:

1. The *direct effects* process suggests that children and adults who watch a lot of media violence may become more aggressive and may develop favorable attitudes and values about the use of aggression to resolve conflicts.

2. *Desensitization* suggests that children who watch a lot of violence in the media may become less sensitive to the impact of violence in the real world, become less reactive to the effects of violence such as the pain and suffering of the victims, and generally be tolerant of violence as a normal, expectable part of everyday life.

3. The third effect, the *mean world syndrome*, refers to the phenomena that individuals who watch a great deal of violence in the media come to view the world as a dangerous place, similar to how the world is portrayed in the media.

4. Particularly troublesome for youth is that those who are exposed to a great deal of violence in the media tend to *view violence and aggression as acceptable* ways to resolve conflicts and solve problems, particularly when one can do it without empathy for the victim and without the expectation of much consequence for their behavior.

Television

Television consumes a large portion of our daily lives. Children in the United States view about two and a half hours of television per day by the time they enter elementary school, increasing their viewing to almost four hours per day by early adolescence, and averaging somewhere between two and three hours during their teenage years.[9] Because children spend so much of their time watching television, it must be considered as one medium that provides a significant source of exposure to violence (in addition to the Internet, computer video games, and games on DVD).

In 1992, the American Psychological Association concluded that, on average, American children had witnessed 8,000 murders by the time they graduated from elementary school and had witnessed more than 100,000 other acts of violence.[10] For each hour of prime-time programming, it is estimated that there occur at least eight acts of violence. Saturday-morning programming is even worse, averaging about twenty to twenty-five violent acts per hour (remember the Roadrunner cartoons and Wile E. Coyote?) Cable television adds to the level of violence exposure through new, more violent programs, easier access, and the recycling of older violent broadcasts. The most violent time periods for cable shows are between 6 and 9 a.m. and between 2 and 5 p.m., the two times of day children are most likely to be watching television. By all accounts, the amount of violence children and adolescents are viewing on television is on the rise, with little evidence that it will abate anytime soon.

In addition to these general effects of exposure to media violence, Comstock and Paik (1991) summarized the evidence for the effects of film or television violence:

- Those who act aggressively or violently get rewarded for their behavior or often do not get punished for their inappropriate behavior.

- There are few consequences for the violent behavior, which is also portrayed without much critical commentary.

- The aggressive behavior is seen as justified.

- The violence portrayed is made to look as similar to real life as possible.

- Situations are set up so that it is easy for children to identify with the aggressor.

- Depictions of violence leave the viewer in a state of arousal and frustration.[11]

Many studies over the past forty years have demonstrated a strong and consistent relationship between watching violence on TV and both immediate and later aggressive, violent behavior.[12] Most studies have examined the effects of watching dramatic violence on TV and film, although a few studies have been observational in nature. One of the earliest studies of TV and aggression involved showing preschool-age children action-oriented aggressive television shows and then placing them in a room with a variety of toys and observing their play. The researchers in those early studies observed that children who watched aggressive shows engaged in a variety of behaviors suggesting an immediate, short-term effect on aggressive behavior compared to children who watched shows with milder content: they kicked and fought with their playmates more, they chose to play with guns and knives more frequently, and they vigorously beat the stuffing out of the Bobo dolls.

Long-term studies have also shown that exposure to media violence can predispose youth to engage in aggressive and violent behavior.[13] Most researchers agree that watching violence in the media does not *cause* an otherwise healthy and well-adjusted child to go out and act violently, but they also agree that watching violence in the media can predispose an already at-risk child (who may be dealing with a host of other problems related to risk for aggression and violence) to act in aggressive and violent ways. These effects have been shown to be both immediate (i.e., shortly after being exposed to violence in the media) and long-term (i.e., TV-violence viewing at ages six to ten is related to adult aggressive behavior and violence fifteen years later). Whereas the early research following youth in the 1960s showed long-term associations for males only, more recent studies that followed youth growing up in the 1970s and 1980s showed the effect for both boys and girls. This is at least indirect evidence for the contention that the content of our TV shows and other media, as well as the overall amount of exposure that children get to violence in the media, has grown substantially over the last couple of decades, and that these early exposures significantly affect later behavior, especially for youth already at risk for problem-behavior outcomes.

How does this happen over time? Most theories suggest that several factors converge to increase the risk for later aggression and violence, with exposure to violence in the media playing a significant role as one of the many other risk factors. We've already summarized the overall effects of violent media on cognition and emotion, but we can add to that a tendency to learn, over time, from observing how those depicted in the media act toward each other. Children are more likely to imitate specific behaviors they see (compared to adults, who may be generally influenced by something but don't always go out and specifically imitate the exact same behavior), both literally through play and also through fantasy. Children are also more likely to identify with aggressive characters who engage in violent behavior, and they are more prone to gradually believe that aggression is a normal, acceptable way to solve problems.

A very recent study showed a strong association between how much television children watch between the ages of one and three and later risk (at age seven) for significant attention problems, including ADHD.[14] Frequent television viewers in early childhood (defined in the study as more than two hours per day for the infants and toddlers) were the most likely to score in the highest 10 percent for concentration problems, impulsive ness, and restlessness, as rated by their mothers at age seven. This doesn't mean that every child in the top 10 percent had ADHD, but youth who struggle with attention and impulsivity in class often experience other learning or behavior problems in school. More television viewing meant more risk. For every extra hour of daily TV watching, a child's risk of having attention problems increased by about 10 percent. For example, kids who watched about three hours of TV per day were 30 percent more likely to have attention problems than were kids who watched no daily television. One concern, according to the study's authors, is that later attention problems may be related to changes in brain structure and neurochemistry that can occur with so much fast-paced, highly stimulating, and unrealistic television viewing by young children with developing brains.

Violent Video Games

One positive development in the media industry is the increased attempt to provide ratings for the content of different mediums like video games, movies, and computer discs of various songs. This rating system has helped us to decide what is an appropriate computer or Play Station 2 video game for our ten-year-old son Joseph, but this hasn't stopped him from trying to get around the system. One day he approached me, casually of course, and said he was interested in purchasing the new video game *Grand Theft Auto 2*, because he had heard it was cool and because "all the other kids have it." Well, I knew I was in for a long discussion. Joe and I began talking about why he wanted to get the game, while I countered with all the reasons he shouldn't have it: it was violent, it was rated for older kids, there was absolutely no socially redeemable value of his getting it, it cost too much, and how was he going to pay for it, because there was no way I was going to pay for such a violent game out of my pocket. Joe persisted. I even tried to change the conversation, asking him if he had any questions about sex that I could answer (which was met with the inevitable "Daaaad").

Then Joe brought out the big guns (no pun intended): "Dad, I play violent video games at my friends' houses all the time, and you don't see me going around beating people up, do you?" Well, he had a point there, but how much is too much? And, while I can't always be there with him when he's at a friend's house playing those games, I want him to be making good decisions about what he does when we're not around, and it's important for him to know how we feel about these things and what rules and boundaries we will have in our house. "Joe," I said, with that concerned, serious look on my face, "you might not play this game and immediately go out and get into a fight, but I notice that when you play a game, you get really hyped up and excited when you play it. Think about how you get into screaming and moving around when you play Madden Football. How do you think you'll get when you play this even more violent, action-packed game than football?"

This got Joe to thinking, and at least he had paused his constant stream of reasons why he was right and I was wrong, claiming I was just overreacting like I always do to these things. Then it hit me—the closer. Use the younger siblings!

"Joe, who is usually standing there right next to you, watching you play your video games every time?"

To this, Joe was perplexed; then the slow recognition and acceptance of defeat crept across his face. "Patrick and Ellen," he replied.

"Yes, Joe, they are always right there watching you play, and sooner or later they want to play with you, right?"

"Yeah, Dad, but how about if I don't let them play?"

"Well, even if they aren't playing and they're just watching you, how do you think they will be able to handle watching all that violence and killing and blood and shooting?" I asked.

"Probably not very well," he admitted. "But Dad, it's not real"—one last attempt to appeal to reason.

"Joe, do you think Ellen knows it's not all real? She's only five. What happens when she lies down with you at night in the basement and you guys are watching a scary movie?"

"She has trouble falling asleep," Joe admitted.

"Do you think she'd have trouble falling asleep if she was standing there watching you play this kind of video game all the time?"

"Yeah, Dad."

I had done it. I had climbed the mountain and had passed over the threshold of defeat. Joe gave in. Of course, he was half the equation, and he could have persisted or just stormed away in disagreement, but to his credit, we had an actual conversation about something that was important to him, and he bought my reasoning, not for himself, but for his younger brother and sister. Sometimes the "No, because I said so" strategy won't work, and one has to appeal to reason and discussion. Sometimes that won't work either, but in this case it helped. It also helped that Joseph was willing to talk to me about it, and I guess that I was willing to talk to him about it. We'll see what happens the next time he brings up wanting to buy the next version of *Grand Theft Auto*.

This incident with Joe brings up an emerging concern about violent video and computer games. It may be one set of problems when children view violence on television and in movies, but this is a rather passive activity, watching the violence unfold on screen in front of you. Playing a violent video game or computer game seems to be a much more active and participatory activity. Will this have a different effect on children, either in the immediate situation or over the long term? Much remains to be learned, but there is more research being done on youth who play violent, action-packed video games and on how playing these games affects different regions of the child's brain, brain chemistry, and circuitry. Whatever happened to *Pacman* and *Pong*?

CHAPTER SIX

THE CHALLENGE OF ADOLESCENCE: WHAT'S ALL THE STORM AND STRESS ABOUT?

A dolescence is a time when many changes occur for children and families. Children look different physically as hormones begin to make them appear more like adults and drive them to seek out sexual experiences. They feel different emotionally and are more up and down on a day-to-day basis. Sometimes they feel happy, sometimes they feel sad, and oftentimes they can't tell you why they feel one way or the other. Adolescents are more likely to be depressed, and most will at least think about hurting or killing themselves at some point. Socially, families (and in particular parents) seem to lose a great deal of influence at the expense of peers. All of a sudden your adolescent wants to be left alone, and then he wants to go be with his friends. Anything is better than hanging out with the family. They begin dating. For some things, the opinion of their friends is really all that matters, but for others, they still depend on the advice and direction of their parents. Adolescents are different cognitively because they are now more able to think in abstract terms, to solve more complex problems, to take the perspective of others, and to reason at a higher moral and ethical level than they could before (which doesn't mean they choose to reason at a higher level, of course). Brain development, as recent research has shown, continues to occur throughout adolescence and into young adulthood. Adolescents begin a more intense process of becoming independent and finding their identity, and they struggle to decide where they fit in life and where they want to go.

Adolescence is a time of many changes and challenges, but it is not a time of inevitable storm and stress. In fact, intense conflict between

TOURO COLLEGE LIBRARY

parents and adolescents characterizes only some families most of the time, even though all parents and adolescents fight at least some of the time. What do they fight about? They fight about the same stuff today as they did a hundred years ago. Parents argue with their adolescent children about keeping their room clean, about taking out the garbage, about picking up their shoes, about taking a shower sometime this week. Parents and adolescents are much more likely to argue about daily, mundane things than they are about the hot topics like religion or politics. When do the problems peak? Conflict between parents and adolescents increases steadily in frequency and intensity from about age ten to around the age of sixteen or seventeen, but then it seems to decline back to preadolescent levels around age eighteen or nineteen. How can this be? One factor is that many children leave home around age eighteen or nineteen, either to go to college or to move off on their own. Being away from their parents essentially gives adolescents and parents less opportunity to argue over the daily things that push their buttons. Of course, the frequency of adolescents leaving home in their late teens has begun to change over the last decade, with more youth living at home for a longer period of time, mostly for financial reasons. Another trend (scary to most parents, anyway) is the increasing frequency with which older adolescents and young adults are moving back into their homes, as their prospects for jobs and financial security are increasingly less stable.

Adolescence is also a time when significant change occurs in the type and frequency of an individual's exposure to violence. Risk for interpersonal or relationship violence with peers is higher just because adolescents are spending more of their time with same-age peers, and they are increasingly involved in intimate relationships with other adolescents. Substance use increases an adolescent's risk for victimization from violence, as does increased access to weapons and opportunities for engaging in delinquent or other types of problem behaviors. Adolescents are exposed more frequently to gangs and gang activity than are younger children and may become involved in gangs themselves, increasing their chances of being exposed to violence (as witness or victim). While all children experience puberty and adolescence differently (and many handle the transition quite well), there are some consistent themes of development that are particularly relevant to mental health and violence exposure and victimization.

Puberty

The most notable change that occurs during adolescence is the onset of puberty. Everybody goes through it sooner or later. Puberty brings with it changes in physical stature, a growth spurt, changes in one's voice and facial features, and the emergence of secondary sex characteristics (i.e., the physical changes you can see). For girls, this means breast development and a widening of the hips. For boys, it usually means more muscle, a broadening of the shoulders, and facial hair. Along with these physical changes come shifts in how we interact with others around us. This happens partly because we feel different, but it also happens because as children begin to physically look older, others begin to expect them to act older. The conundrum is that early adolescents are rarely up to the task cognitively, emotionally, or socially.

One of the most widely researched aspects of the physical changes of puberty has been the timing of physical maturation. We know that everybody goes through puberty in roughly the same sequence of physical changes. We also know that the hormonal and chemical changes that eventually emerge as secondary sex characteristics begin internally for most youth around the age of nine or ten. What seems to matter quite a bit is whether a child experiences puberty early, on time, or late compared to his or her peer group.

Why is the timing of puberty so important? Let's agree that, in general, youth who are on time and generally go through puberty with the rest of their same-age peers tend to do the best overall emotionally and socially. This is not to say that just because an adolescent is on time he won't experience difficulties in adolescence. Far from it, but being either early or late compared to one's same-age friends does appear to be an additional significant risk factor for problem behavior and social-emotional development.

The challenges related to being a late-onset maturer in puberty are fairly well documented. The child who matures after everyone else stands out noticeably in a crowd. For boys, this means they are shorter, weaker, and baby faced longer than their peers. Males place a great deal of importance on athleticism as a measure of popularity, so the late-maturing male is at a significant disadvantage socially compared to his friends. Physically smaller boys are also more likely to be harassed and victimized by bullies than other boys. For females, late-onset puberty means breasts don't develop at the same time as all the other girls are developing. It means that boys aren't paying as much attention. Girls also struggle with being popular. A female doesn't suffer in quite the same way athletically as her late-maturing male friend (e.g., girls who stay competitive in dance or gymnastics longer because of a delayed onset of puberty), but this trend is also changing as female athletic programs are gaining in stature and intensity. In general, being a late maturer is more difficult than being on time and can be related to increased social isolation and problems with body image, self-concept, and moodiness. In the long run, however, most kids who are late maturers tend to adjust once they go through puberty, and they go on to be productive, happy adults.

Early maturing youth face a different array of challenges. For males, being an early maturer can lead to great success in athletics, which is closely tied to being popular. I remember all of the discussion among my male friends about who had to shave first and who had the most underarm hair. This usually moved on to comparisons of how much weight one could lift or how far one could throw a football or hit a baseball. It was clear to everyone in sixth and seventh grade who the early maturers were among the boys and the girls. The boys were the star athletes, and the girls were the ones that all the guys (particularly the star athletes) wanted to date. What happens socially to early maturing males? While they enjoy early popularity and garner lots of attention, it is the rare male who is able to handle all of this later on when the adulation recedes as others catch up to him or when he finally begins to struggle with academics because he spent all of his time on sports and hanging out with his friends. How many athletic stars from your high school, who were popular and were given lots of advantages but who also struggled academically, have gone on to achieve great things later in life? Some have, but many others have struggled, for a variety of reasons.

For females, being an early maturer brings much attention, mostly from older boys. Early-maturing females often struggle because they begin hanging out with these older boys, who are not much interested in stimulating conversation. Early-maturing girls are generally not yet able to emotionally or socially handle the increased pressures of dating older boys, and neither can they navigate the situations that present themselves when a fifteen-year-old girl is hanging out with eighteen- and nineteen-year-old boys.

The research on pubertal timing consistently shows that early maturers, both boys and girls, are at increased risk for engaging in a whole host of problem behaviors. These include early sexual activity, experimentation with and use of drugs, becoming involved in delinquent behavior, and academic failure. The disconnect between early physical development and lagging cognitive, social, and emotional development is too much to handle for many youth, who are also struggling with changes in hormones and brain chemistry, the expectations of others, peer pressure, being on an emotional roller coaster, increased conflict with parents, struggles over achieving autonomy, increasingly complex school work, finding a part-time job, and finding an identity.

Cognitive Development

Cognitive maturity is a tricky thing in adolescence. New research is continuing to demonstrate that adolescent brains continue to grow neurons and prune away the connections that are not being actively used. Magnetic resonance imaging (MRI) studies show us how different parts of an adolescent's brain are activated by stimulation from the environment, and which parts heat up when adolescents undertake different types of intellectual tasks. For many years, we held to the model that cognitive development occurred in a very structured, ordered way, with the highest levels of maturation occurring in late adolescence, when most of us finally have the ability to think abstractly and to take the perspective of others, critical features of problem solving, social skill development, moral reasoning, empathy, and impulse control.

In the last twenty years or so, new theories of intellectual development have emerged, some that model thinking skills after the way a computer handles information, from very basic input to more complex metacognitive processing skills. We understand that people encode, pay attention to, and retrieve information with a variety of different techniques and with varying degrees of efficiency and success. We understand that individuals learn material and are motivated to achieve in vastly different ways. Other theories have emerged about social intelligence and emotional IQ. There is growing recognition that intelligence is not limited to how well one can define words or how fast one can construct puzzles with colored blocks, but that it includes how fluent a person is in her thinking, how flexible she is in choosing from options and alternatives in problem solving, or how she acts in a social situation. Intelligence is still viewed as a fairly stable trait that doesn't change dramatically from middle childhood unless there is some unusual incident, illness, or brain injury that causes significant problems with how an individual is able to process, store, and retrieve information.

One of the most interesting concepts regarding cognitive development is the "necessary-but-not-sufficient" criterion. In brief, this criterion asserts that in order for a person to be able to reason at a particular level of moral reasoning or empathy, he must first possess the ability to think abstractly and the ability to take the perspective of another person. The reason these skills are necessary is that one cannot possibly behave in a morally acceptable, universal manner with the common good in mind unless he has the cognitive skills to do so. The reason these skills are not sufficient in and of themselves is that just because one has the ability to think empathically about the well-being of others, this does not mean he will do so (think of siblings who fight with each other).

Perhaps an example will help illustrate the point. In our society, we have rules and laws that people are expected to follow to maintain order and fairness. Most people would agree that it would be wrong to steal something from another person. But what if stealing something is done to save the life of another person? Does the higher-order good (saving a life) justify breaking the law? This is a type of moral dilemma. It is the kind of dilemma that we use to assess a person's level of moral reasoning. Most children operate at a fairly low level. They know as toddlers when they do something bad, but mostly because of the reactions of others when they do it (I'm reminded of the book *No, David!* by David Shannon),[1] not because they understand that it is wrong to take a cookie from someone else. As children, they go through a law-and-order orientation. While they understand that there are laws and rules, they believe it is really only a problem if they get caught. This is why a child's older sibling will accuse her of a misdeed when something bad happens. It's OK to blame someone else as long as you don't get caught. This is also the level at which most delinquent adolescents think.

As children get older, they develop more mature thinking and reasoning skills that allow them to begin to understand that it is not right to hurt another person on purpose, that there is a reason why we stop at red lights, and that while a shopkeeper may have more money than we do, it is not fair to him or others or to society if we were to go into his store and take something without paying for it. By adolescence, most individuals have developed the *capacity* to reason at a higher moral level. They will argue with their parents and peers that it is OK to protest and sit in the streets because people are starving in other parts of the world. Getting arrested (breaking the law) at a nuclear protest is OK because nuclear proliferation is universally unacceptable.

Along with cognitive maturity comes the ability to take the perspective of others, an important facet of social interaction and problem solving. A long-researched phenomenon unique to the teen years is called adolescent egocentrism. Being egocentric in adolescence generally refers to two phenomena: (1) a heightened sense of self-consciousness (the imaginary audience) and (2) a sense of indestructibility and uniqueness, the belief that "it won't happen to me" (the personal fable). The imaginary audience might help explain why some adolescents spend hours worried about what they will wear. When they go to a party and spill mustard on their shirt, they are convinced that everyone else will see it and make a big deal out of it. This self-consciousness and anxiety over what others will think (because obviously everyone is paying attention to them) can have a big influence on behaviors in social settings with peers. The personal fable is more directly related to becoming involved in risky, problem behaviors like early sexual activity, driving while drinking, or racing the train to the intersection. Most adolescents believe they will live forever and that they are invincible. They can drink and drive, and nothing bad will happen. They can try the drug only once; what's the big deal? The personal fable can increase the chances that an adolescent will take risks that most of us wouldn't even consider.

You Got a Problem with Me?

One troubling aspect of the violence that young people engage in these days is how it is characterized by a lack of empathy for others and is laced with a sense of hopelessness about one's future and a lack of any sense of control or efficacy about what will happen to them. Violence seems to be more impulsive and reactionary than it used to be. Adolescents are much more likely to react in an aggressive and violent manner to a perceived slight or the belief that they are being disrespected in front of their friends. Peer pressure aside, many adolescents report reacting aggressively or violently simply because someone else looked at them funny.

This increase in impulsive, reactive violence can be partly traced back to brain development and to more and more children growing up in chronically violent environments, as victims and witnesses to unpredictable, chronic violence. Not only is their exposure to violence more frequent, but the violence seems to be escalating in intensity, lethality, and immediacy. Recent research on brain development shows how these kinds of exposures can be rewarding to the brain because the mechanisms for novelty seeking in adolescent brains are much more active than the ability to control impulses or regulate emotion.[2]

For example, children whose development is filled with experiences of a chronic state of stress and fear will grow up with brains that are much more likely to be wired for hypervigilance and impulsive reactions to threatening stimuli. This is a survival instinct that becomes ingrained due to repeated exposure to the same environmental threats over time. The problem is complicated by cognitive distortions of neutral or ambiguous stimuli in their environment. Things that aren't clear are more likely to be perceived as threatening, and aggressive youth are likely to react to this ambiguity with impulsive anger, hostility, or violence. These youth exist in a persistent state of physiological hyperarousal and hyperactivity. Mental health issues (e.g., depression, anxiety, anger) often contribute to these misattributions, or at least to the adolescent's inability to respond appropriately in these varied social situations.

A few examples might help illustrate how problems with misattributions about what is going on in the environment can lead to an increased risk for aggression and violence. Two adolescent boys are walking in opposite directions down a crowded hallway at school in between classes. This tends to be a relatively frenzied time in most schools, with lots of noise, disorganized hallways, and little adult monitoring of what's going on. Let's say the two boys accidentally bump into each other as their paths cross. One of the two boys has a reputation of being a bully at school, of verbally harassing the females, and of occasionally demanding lunch money from his smaller, less assertive peers. Immediately upon dropping his books on the floor, the aggressive boy stops and shouts at the other boy, "Hey, what did you do that for?" and shoves the other boy. The other boy meekly replies, "It was an accident, man. I didn't do it on purpose." Of course, the aggressive boy barely hears any of this response, as he is already physically attacking the other boy, pounding on him with his fists as he escalates his own rage against his perceived assailant.

What is going on here? First, the aggressive boy is walking down the hallway in a state of hypervigilance in the first place. When the other boy bumps into him, he is much more likely to misinterpret the bump as something the other boy did on purpose. In other words, he cognitively misattributes the other boy's intent (it was on purpose) and his behavior (he was trying to hurt me). The problem is compounded because, immediately upon making the misattribution, the aggressive boy is less likely to have the ability to think very quickly about what to do in the situation. This is the fluidity of thought, referring to how quickly the boy is able to generate various solutions to a particular problem situation. The aggressive boy is also not very flexible in his thinking, referring to how good he is at choosing a solution to the problem that will be appropriate and will lead to a positive resolution. Lastly, since he is by nature more impulsive in his behavior and less empathic toward others, he is much more likely to act aggressively without thinking and without caring very much about whether he hurts the other person or gets in trouble himself for getting into a fight. The main focus is on how he was hurt and disrespected, so now he has no other choice but to fight back. He may even believe it is his right to fight back under these circumstances.

A different example might also apply here. I often participate in the training of police officers regarding their understanding of youth development and how they interact with young people in nonarrest situations. As part of this training, we talk about the impact of violence on adolescents and about the fact that many aggressive, violent youth might misattribute the way an officer approaches or speaks to him. Young people may react in impulsive, defensive, or aggressive ways, especially if they are standing around with some of their friends. To illustrate this point about misattributions, I sometimes, without warning in the middle of a sentence about something else, stop what I am saying. I then quickly turn toward an officer with a disgusted, stern look on my face and ask, "Hey, you got a problem with what I'm saying? You got a problem with me? You want to take this outside right now?" Most officers are a bit startled by this but will usually stammer out some reply. Everyone around them watches while the officer becomes increasingly uncomfortable and defensive, and the longer I draw it out, the more agitated the target of my hostility becomes. I use this little interaction to illustrate the point about cognitive misattributions, about how misinterpreting the way someone is looking at you can lead to aggressive interactions when they don't have to.

During one training, I turned to a middle-aged officer among a group of command-level staff in a large, urban police department. I went into my little unannounced role-play, and the officer sat there, silent, just staring back at me. Since he wasn't saying anything, I kept going and pressing him, acting like I was increasingly upset and agitated. The whole interaction probably only lasted about two minutes, but after the third or fourth insult I posed to him, he began to slowly rise out of his seat, leaning across the table toward me. Fortunately, I quickly ended the little interaction to the "oohs" among his fellow commanders (all of whom were armed, of course). I explained to the group what I was doing, but the lieutenant did not appear to be taking the "harassment" lightly, and he sat there until the next break with a disconcerted, nasty look on his face.

Once we took a break, he immediately came up to me and pulled me aside. One of my fellow trainers came over, thinking retaliation might be about to occur. On the contrary, the lieutenant began telling me an interesting tale. He said that as soon as I approached him in a threatening manner, he immediately tuned out the rest of the room and was "back in Vietnam," unaware of his surroundings. He told me that if I had not broken off the interaction when I did, he probably would have gone over the table at me and would have tried to hurt me in any way he could, fearing for his own safety. He recounted some of the traumatic memories he was experiencing (in fact reexperiencing) and how he felt he was physically and emotionally back in Vietnam, with the same fear, survival instincts, and reactions that had helped him then. He agreed to bring this back to the group, which was hard-pressed to believe our brief interaction could have taken him back nearly thirty years to all of the same emotional and physical reactions he didn't feel were completely under his control in that training room. Because he was a respected officer, his colleagues eventually came to understand his reaction, why and how it occurred. They also began to tell stories of how they had experienced similar reactions to threatening, stressful events (with the same behavioral and mental health consequences) in the course of their policing careers.

While this story in and of itself may be interesting, the ending was even more poignant. Several weeks later, I ran into the lieutenant in an elevator at police headquarters. Days earlier, he was called to the scene of a domestic incident in which an adult male assailant was holding a weapon against a female victim. In the course of responding to the incident, after much negotiation with the perpetrator, the lieutenant was forced to discharge his weapon and seriously injure the assailant. What he said to me was that had he not had the experience he had had in the course of the training, he probably would have acted much more impulsively and aggressively, probably killing the perpetrator and potentially hurting the female victim. Further, after the shooting occurred, he said he had a much better understanding of how the traumatic event was going to affect his behavior and his mental health, so he was in a much better position to cope with it effectively.

From Parents to Peers

Developmentally, we know that during adolescence youth spend more time with peers than they do with their parents or other family members. This is often fodder for many family conflicts. While most adolescents report that they prefer to be with their friends versus their family, they also admit that parents in particular continue to exert a significant influence in their lives. Adolescents report that while peers may influence what they do on a daily basis, who is in their larger group of friends, how they dress, and what they eat, they still depend on their parent's value system as an important guide and continue to value their parent's opinion on a whole host of important issues. Even the small stuff matters. For instance, according to one large national study, adolescents were less likely to get into trouble, over a long period of time, if they had parents who verbally told them they disapproved of that behavior. All parents had to do was tell their adolescent that it was inappropriate, wrong, or not good for them to try illegal substances, and adolescents were significantly less likely to engage in that behavior compared to their friends who could not report ever hearing this from one of their parents.

Parents and adolescents also get into more fights about more stuff than younger and older kids do. Part of the explanation for this may be that the way parents communicate with their adolescent changes from when children were younger. When we videotaped parents and their early adolescents in conversations about things they argued about and things they enjoyed doing together, we found several unique features about the way they discussed and sometimes resolved issues.[3] First, we noticed that parents and adolescents were much more likely to express emotion via mixed or sarcastic messages that were not always easy to interpret. An example of a mixed message would be saying something nice to one's adolescent (positive content) with a sarcastic voice (negative voice tone) or saying "Nice job!" while rolling one's eyes (negative nonverbal behavior). These mixed messages were much more common in the communication patterns of adolescents and their parents than they were between younger children and parents. Second, we found that conversations became not only more negative but also significantly less positive as adolescents physically matured (as compared to finding more negative but that the positive affect remained steady). Last, when we looked at how satisfied adolescents were with their relationships with parents, it was the father's expression of negative emotion in conversations that carried the most weight in influencing relationship satisfaction. In other words, adolescents whose fathers expressed high negative affect in conversations rated the overall relationship quality to be lower. Either adolescents are just used to more yelling from their mothers, or fathers are less likely to talk to their adolescents, so when they do (and they are clear in expressing their support or their displeasure), adolescents are more likely to listen.

Pressure from peers to engage in inappropriate behavior, including experimentation with tobacco, alcohol, and other drugs, also increases significantly in adolescence. Peer influence is a particular problem for young people if their peer group largely consists of other kids who do not do well in school (or have already dropped out) or if their friends are regularly engaged in delinquent behavior. From a sociological perspective, several prominent theories of offending point to the role of peer influence and to the opportunities that associating with a deviant peer group pose as significant risk factors in whether a young person will engage in delinquency or violence.

While peers gain influence, many adolescents also recognize the importance of institutions like school and religion. Intellectually, most adolescents understand that staying in school is important, while they may struggle with being able to appreciate the long-term consequences of academic failure. Most adolescents also report an appreciation for the role that religion plays in their life, and if they are not consistently involved in some sort of religious activity (like going to church on Sundays), they usually report that they would like to do more of it and that they think it would help them. This is a positive finding, particularly in light of the increased trend of utilizing faith-based organizations in work with at-risk youth.

Additional information on adolescent health is available from the National Longitudinal Study of Adolescent Health (Add Health), conducted out of the University of North Carolina. This large study gathered survey and interview data from thousands of adolescents and their parents from around the country. The researchers have gathered information on a very diverse group of adolescents: youth from across geographic settings (urban, suburban, and rural communities), from various racial and ethnic groups, and from all socioeconomic levels. Data from the Add Health study has just begun showing up in the scientific literature in the last couple of years, and its findings have provided much insight into what is happening with adolescent behavior, mental health, and academic achievement. The study is a comprehensive assessment of risk and protective factors related to a wide range of adolescent outcomes, including substance use, violence, mental health, school performance, and teen pregnancy. Findings from the Add Health study are accessible via the Internet at http://cpc.unc.edu/projects/addhealth.

Dating Violence

Ask any adolescents about date rape, and they could probably tell you about someone they know who was victimized or who was forced to participate in a sexual act against his or her will. Most adolescents who report experience with dating violence report being both a victim and a perpetrator.[4] Estimates of the prevalence of dating violence vary but generally hover around 20 percent, with some studies showing different rates depending on whether one surveys adolescents in urban, suburban, or rural communities. In any event, about one in five adolescents will report being victimized by dating violence, and a higher percentage will report being forced to do something physically or sexually that they were uncomfortable doing. Psychological abuse usually occurs before physical violence. Talk with your adolescent about this as soon as he or she begins dating. Your child needs to know what is appropriate, how to establish clear expectations and boundaries with a dating partner, and what to do if something inappropriate happens. Don't leave them guessing. Make sure they know you will be there to help them and support them whenever they need it.

Gangs and Violence

One particularly unique phenomenon to early and middle adolescence is an increased risk for exposure to and involvement in gangs and gang-related activity. There continues to exist a great deal of controversy over what actually constitutes a gang, but there is even more concern over why kids end up joining gangs and, if they ever want to get out of a gang, how they can do that.

Gangs are usually (but not always) characterized by groups of youth with some formal organizational structure with an identified leader or hierarchy, and the group is often identified with a specific territory or turf. A gang's behavior or activity is sometimes characterized by delinquent or criminal acts, which is the criterion that sets gangs apart from more prosocial adolescent peer groups. Who belongs to gangs? Members typically range in age from about fourteen to twenty-four, with the peak age of membership around seventeen, but some studies have identified children as young as eight as gang involved, and many prisons and communities are replete with older adults still actively involved in gang life. Most large-scale surveys indicate that anywhere from 5 to 8 percent of adolescents are at high risk for being involved in gangs.

In research conducted with my colleague Ronald Huff, we identified a developmental progression from hanging out with the gang (i.e., being a gang wannabe) to joining the gang and getting arrested.[5] Most members first begin associating with a gang around the age of thirteen and join, on average, about six months later. The age of first arrest is about fourteen, approximately one year after beginning to associate with a gang. Arrest for property crimes seems to peak about one to two years before arrests for either drug offenses or violent crimes. Rather than gang membership providing protection, Huff found that a high percentage of gang leaders' declining arrest rates was due to incarceration and death. While gangs are still dominated by males, female gang membership (and rates of violence among female gang members) is rising more quickly than among males.

What are the benefits of being in a gang? For some youth, being accepted and belonging to a group that provides a great deal of social support is a powerful motivator. Many youth report joining gangs because of significant abuse or rejection at home. For some youth who live in disorganized, chaotic, and high-crime neighborhoods, gangs offer a social outlet with peers who face the same dire conditions, a sort of misery-loves-company phenomenon. One real pragmatic benefit of being a gang member is related to criminal activity. We have found that adolescents involved in a gang make considerably more money per transaction of selling a drug than do non-gang-involved youth (by as much as 50 percent more in earnings per week). While not all gangs are involved in the drug business, when they are, there appears to be a real economic benefit of being in a gang, and because you can make more money per transaction, you also reduce your risk of being caught selling.

What do gang-involved youth do compared to non-gang-involved youth? In our survey of how youth spend their time, we found striking similarities between the daily activities of gang and non-gang youth. Non-gang youth are more likely to be involved in sporting activities than are gang-involved youth, while gang members are significantly more likely to party; attend musical concerts; hang out; cruise for members of the opposite sex; engage in fighting (including violent fighting like drive-by shootings and homicides), drinking, drug use, and drug sales; and put up and cross out graffiti. Despite these differences, there were many more similarities between how gang and non-gang youth report spending their time.

Being in a gang places a youth at higher risk for exposure to violence, victimization from violence, and opportunities (and sometimes pressure) to offend and engage in aggressive, delinquent, and violent behavior. They are also at heightened risk for experiencing serious mental health problems. Gang youth report more frequent thinking about suicide and more attempts to hurt themselves. Youth involved in gangs also report higher levels of substance use compared to youth not involved in gangs. Their long-term outlook is not positive. For both boys and girls, being involved in a gang is related to earlier onset of sexual intercourse, unsafe sex, and early pregnancy or fathering of a child. Active gang members do not live as long as their non-gang-involved peers, and if they do live into adulthood and are not incarcerated, they usually obtain lower-paying, less satisfying jobs (partly due to lower academic achievement). While gang-involved youth are more likely to report having been involved in homicides and other violence, it is important to note here that most gang-related homicides are over turf battles, not drugs.

Drugs, Firearms, and Violence

Substance use and firearms both increase the risk of serious violence. Research has consistently shown that having access to a firearm increases the risk of suicide, accidental shootings, and using a firearm to settle a dispute with another person.[6] If there has been one constant over the past two decades in our understanding of youth violence, it is that substance use and firearms have contributed significantly to the increased rate of homicide perpetration and victimization among young people.[7] Fights that used to be settled with fists are now more likely to be settled using a lethal weapon. Youth who are depressed and are under the influence of alcohol are more likely to use a weapon to take their own life. Adolescents use drugs or alcohol as a vehicle to allow them to go out and commit acts of violence against others. One of the main reasons our homicide rate hasn't skyrocketed further has been the dramatic improvement in emergency and trauma medical services. For every fatal homicide by a firearm, estimates are that there are at least another five nonfatal injuries. As it is, the homicide rate due to firearms among youth younger than age twenty-five in the United States far outpaces the rate of homicide in any other industrialized country. For most other countries, the homicide rate for youth hovers at its highest around 3 to 5 per 100,000. In the United States, the rate is as high as 22 per 100,000, depending on the age group examined (nearly five times higher than any other country).[8] Put another way, in the 1990s, youth in the United States accounted for three out of every four homicides among children in twenty-six different countries.[9] When one looks only at youth homicides due to firearms, the United States is the clear winner, with death rates nearly sixteen times higher than all of the other countries combined.[10]

Why do youth carry guns? Some research points to the feelings of power, control, and authority that come with carrying a firearm. Most youth will say they are carrying a weapon for protection and not with the intent to use it, but when they find themselves involved in a potential conflict, having a gun makes it more likely that they will use it against the other person. Weapon carrying is extremely frequent among gang-involved youth and among youth incarcerated as juveniles. About 80 percent of gang-involved youth admit to carrying a concealed weapon, and over half of all incarcerated juveniles admit that they have regularly carried a gun in the past year. This compares to just over 10 percent of youth who admit to bringing a gun to school at some point in the past year, usually citing need for protection. Even more disheartening than the number of youth who carry guns is the data that reflects how easy it is for someone to acquire a gun, legally or illegally. In most surveys of high school students, only about one-third of students say they would have any difficulty in getting a gun if they wanted one. They would "borrow" one from a friend or relative, or they know how they could purchase one on the street or from a peer. In the end, only one common theme emerges: guns and drugs go together, and their combination often produces a volatile mix of fear and violence.

What is the relationship between substance use in adolescence and mental health? A significant proportion of adolescent suicide attempts occur while the youth is under the influence of alcohol or other drugs. Many adolescents use drugs to self-medicate, as a way to temporarily get rid of their feelings of depression, anxiety, or stress. Drugs are used as a way to cope with situations that often seem hopeless and futile. Substance use is also a prominent factor in the incidence of violence between intimates, and that includes adolescent relationships. Substance use often coexists with significant mental health problems, but also with serious behavior problems related to violence like conduct disorder, impulse control problems and anger, and antisocial behavior.

How many adolescents are substance users? Our surveys of middle school youth show that about 10 percent of sixth and seventh graders have tried marijuana, and about a third have tried beer, wine, or cigarettes. In annual national surveys, about four in ten high school students report having used marijuana at least once in their lifetime. Rates of use for other illicit drugs among high school students vary widely by geography, gender, and ethnicity, but they range from a couple of percentage points to just over 20 percent of high school students reporting use of at least one illicit drug such as cocaine, methamphetamine, ecstasy, LSD, or heroine. Nearly all adolescents who report illicit drug use also report a significant history of tobacco and alcohol use, so these are consistent gateway risk factors for subsequent illicit drug use. With respect to violence, some innovative studies have shown that weapon carrying and physical fighting are not only associated with alcohol use and illicit substance use but are also highly associated with cigarette smoking.[11]

Like the risk for delinquency and violence, personality factors play a role in who will be a substance user. The earlier the onset of experimentation and use, the more likely an adolescent will progress to serious drug use. Socialization, opportunity, and genetics also play a role. Adolescents who grow up in a household where parents or older siblings are heavy alcohol or drug users are more likely to also use alcohol or drugs than are adolescents who grow up being socialized in a different way. In our own research, we have shown that hanging out with friends who use substances and being susceptible to peer pressure are more significant factors in predicting which early adolescents will use substances than are other family and personality factors typically studied.[12]

The sequence of substance use is fairly well established and pretty consistent across youth, meaning there are very few exceptions to the course of going from experimentation to use and abuse. Most youth start with tobacco as the entry drug, and they start early (about 25 percent have tried cigarettes before the age of thirteen), but this is not confined solely to cigarette use. National surveys are showing increased rates of smokeless tobacco use, both snuff and chewing tobacco, which are just as addictive (and can lead to serious forms of mouth cancer) than cigarette use. After tobacco, youth then experiment with beer or wine before moving on to hard liquor. After hard liquor, youth who progress on will then try marijuana, followed by inhalants or amphetamines. The more illicit drugs follow, and these seem to change in form and function on a regular basis. For a period of time, it may be cocaine that is the drug of choice for illicit users (either crack or powder form), then it seems that youth switch to heroine for a time, and then they switch to methamphetamine or GBH (the date rape drug). Several facts are persistently clear from the research on adolescent substance use: (1) early-onset users (i.e., those who start at a young age) are more likely to progress to more serious substance use and abuse than are youth who begin substance use at a later age; (2) youth who associate with peers who are substance users are at significantly higher risk of also using substances, compared to adolescents whose friends are not drug users; (3) we cannot easily predict who will move from experimentation with a substance to heavy use or abuse and who will experiment and decide that they have no interest in moving on to more illicit substances; and (4) once an adolescent is dependent on a substance due to abuse, getting back to a sober lifestyle is an extremely difficult, long, and painful process that often ends in failure.

Adolescence is a time of many changes and transitions in relationships, physical growth, emotional stability, and intellectual capacity. These many changes can create significant challenge and conflict, but the storm and stress of adolescence you hear about is not inevitable. Being prepared for change is different than expecting the worst as predetermined. Few families report smooth riding; that is for sure. There will be bumps in the road, but most kids don't end up as car wrecks. Occasionally they need servicing, once in a while a tow, and always maintenance to keep them in good running condition. If you really want to be nice to them, clean them up once in a while and take them out for a spin. The road will also have some big hills and unexpected curves, but none that can't be navigated safely with a little attention, a lot of effort, more support than you ever imagined you could give, and the flexibility to deal with all of the unpredictable things that will happen along the way.

CHAPTER SEVEN
ARE SCHOOLS ANY SAFER TODAY? VIOLENCE IN THE EVERYDAY LIVES OF CHILDREN

W e tell children that going to school and doing well is their job. Children and adolescents spend most of their waking hours at school with their peers, with teachers, and with other adults responsible for imparting knowledge and helping them to high levels of academic achievement. We expect children to attend school. In fact, we require it by law and impose consequences (sometimes on parents) if children are persistently truant from school or fail to show up without having a legitimate excuse to miss. Schools, for better or worse, have become ma jor socializing institutions in our society. We expect a great deal from our schools and those who teach within their walls. We expect teachers to be effective in making our children achieve at their highest level of ability. We expect teachers to find ways to motivate our children to do their best, to accommodate their special needs, to pay attention to cultural differences, and to accommodate our personal preferences and wishes for how our children are to be socialized and disciplined. We expect teachers to tell us if our children are different, to tell us if our children need special help, or to let us know if they suspect something bad is happening to them at school, in the neighborhood, or even at home. We expect teachers and schools to be many things to our children, much more than the historical expectation that our children will go to school and learn new things. These days, on top of everything else, we expect our teachers and schools to create a safe and secure learning environment for our children.

What happened to schools being open, welcoming, safe havens for learning and accomplishment? Have things changed gradually over time, or has there been some dramatic shift in the need to focus more heavily on school violence? Some things have been at issue for a long time. For example, some form of violence has always existed in our schools. Violence at schools can include being the victim of a property offense, or it may involve being harassed for lunch money by the bully. It can manifest itself when a child is called names or is rejected by the popular peer group. In some schools, violence is perpetrated by youth who are members of gangs, or violence is characterized by frequent fighting and clashes between groups of students who live in different parts of town or belong to different ethnic groups. For some schools, violence is characterized by a climate of intolerance or by a setting that is disorganized and chaotic. In some schools, hallways, cafeterias, and playgrounds are hot spots where aggression and victimization from violence are common. While various forms of violence have existed in schools ever since children began going to schools on a regular basis, most of us would agree that violence is more common and its outcomes more serious than in the past. How has this come about?

In part, school violence is of greater concern to adults and youth because of the increase in highly publicized shootings and other acts of serious violence at school. These events have received a great deal of media attention (and even some research) in the past decade or so. Most of us can recite the names of the places where the most horrific incidents have occurred: Columbine, Paducah, Springfield, and Jonesboro, to name a few. Recent research has confirmed that the incidence of *multiple* homicide shootings at schools has risen in recent years. This is surely a disturbing trend, and we need to continue to be vigilant about the possibility of repeat events and copycat incidents. Investigations of school violence over many years have also shown, however, that the chance of being a victim of serious violence at school has remained very steady over the past fifty years. So, while the number of dramatic shootings at schools has increased, the overall chance of being a victim of violence, especially homicide, at school has remained extremely low for many years. How low is low? Is any rate of victimization from serious violence at school acceptable?

According to an annual survey of school safety conducted by the U.S. Department of Education, in the year 2000 students between the ages of twelve and eighteen were victims of 1.9 million total crimes, and about

128,000 youth were victims of serious violent crimes at school (e.g., rape, sexual assault, or aggravated assault).[1] In the 1999 Youth Risk Behavior Survey by the Centers for Disease Control (CDC), over 17 percent of youth reported that they had carried a weapon in the past thirty days, with 7 percent reporting they had brought the weapon to school. Between 1993 and 2001, almost 10 percent of students in grades nine through twelve reported that they had been threatened or injured by a weapon on school property within the past twelve months.

While these numbers seem to be quite high (and they are certainly nothing to sneeze at), three observations require mention. First, the rates of serious victimization from violence at school are very low, averaging about 4 percent for high school seniors over the last twenty-five years. Second, the most frequent form of victimization, having something stolen from you at school, has remained very stable over time and has not increased very much from the mid-1970s through today. Thus, despite all of the media perception and hype around multiple homicide incidents at school (which have increased proportionally to other forms of violence at school), the overall rate of victimization from violence at school among high school seniors has not increased. Third, all of the data continue to show that, whatever is going on in schools with respect to violence victimization and perpetration (witnessing violence may be different), rates of violence at school are still significantly lower than what children and adolescents experience at home and in their neighborhoods.

The bottom line is that schools are still very safe places for our children to spend their time. The overall rate of violence in schools has in fact been declining in recent years, and more violence among youth occurs away from school than at school. Despite the declining rate of overall violence, most parents report that they believe schools are less safe than they used to be, and many students feel less safe going to and from school and at school than they used to feel. Some studies estimate that as many as half of all students believe that their school is becoming more violent, and as many as one in five are afraid of being shot or hurt by other students who bring weapons to school. Some children report that they are afraid to go certain places in their school (e.g., the restroom) because they're scared they might be victimized in these unsupervised areas. Despite what the statistics tell us, the perception that schools are less safe than they used to be remains a significant concern, so much so that the government has enacted several laws and initiatives in the past few years to deal specifically with the issue of school violence.

Due to high levels of school violence and the perception that violence at schools is on the rise, school districts and the U.S. government have stressed the importance of violence-free schools in acts such as Goals 2000, the implementation of the Safe Schools/Healthy Students Initiative, and the No Child Left Behind (NCLB) Act of 2001. For example, one of the stated aims of the Goals 2000 initiative is that, "by the year 2000, every school in America will be free of drugs and violence and will offer a disciplined environment conducive to learning." The Safe Schools/Healthy Students initiative was launched in 1999 as a first-ever collaboration among the federal departments of Education, Justice, and Health and Human Services. This collaborative effort awards resources (on a competitive grant basis) to local school districts that are charged with implementing and evaluating the effectiveness of comprehensive services to reduce substance use and violence in their school. The programs that are implemented must be a collaborative effort involving law enforcement and mental health services for youth, a requirement of receiving the funds. School districts must also gather information about what happens to levels of violence and substance use in their schools and among children who receive special services as part of the initiative. Results from the first group of school districts who received funding are just now being shared nationally, with some promising results. Whether the programs will be sustained over time, given the significant cutbacks in funding for schools and reductions in resources at the federal level, remains to be seen.

The No Child Left Behind Act contains specific language about schools having to maintain a climate of safety, and it allows parents to transfer their students to another school should the building they attend experience high rates of crime and violence. Unfortunately, the federal government left standards for academic achievement and safety up to individual states. Whereas rates of academic achievement have been publicly available via student pass rates on standardized tests for years, data on violent incidents at schools is largely kept from public view. No school administrator wants significant publicity over an incident of violence at his or her school. Many potentially violent incidents are handled informally without reporting the incident to police. Many schools also have their own safety and security forces or off-duty police officers monitoring school grounds and hallways, so many incidents are handled internally. While this may be an effective way to intervene with most school-related incidents of aggression, violence, and victimization, it leaves many questions about what is really happening at most of our schools with respect to safety and security. In fact, fewer than one hundred schools nationally met the state definitions of being unsafe based on incidents of violence formally reported during the 2001 school year, and most of those schools were in only two or three locations that reported a handful of schools as currently meeting the criteria for being unsafe. Put another way, over forty-five states reported that they had no schools in the entire state that would be considered unsafe. While the NCLB Act imposed stringent language and accountability standards, there remains much work to be done before school data can be taken seriously as a realistic measure of what is going on with respect to violence.

One way to assess levels of school related violence is to examine rates of the most serious forms of violence like homicide and suicide. A potential fight between two youth, a threat made against a teacher, or the theft of a gym bag can be handled informally or through the school's discipline policy or security force. A homicide or suicide that occurs on school grounds or during a school activity is a more serious event that must be reported to law enforcement authorities. What is a student's risk of being a victim of a homicide at school or committing suicide at school?

In a two-year period (1992 to 1994), 105 school-associated violent deaths were identified by one research team, with about half of the incidents occurring during school hours and half occurring at school-related activities.[2] Between 1994 and 1999, 220 violent incidents at school resulted in 172 homicides, 30 suicides, 11 homicide-suicides, 5 legal intervention deaths, and 2 unintentional firearm deaths, with students accounting for 68 percent of these deaths.[3] Between 1992 and 2001, there were thirty-five incidents in which students showed up at school or school-sponsored events and started shooting at their classmates or teachers. Most national data sets on school-related deaths show that students in urban schools are more likely to be killed violently at school than are students in suburban or rural schools. However, none of the highly publicized multiple school shootings in the past fifteen years has occurred at an urban school; all have taken place in rural (e.g., Jonesboro) or suburban upper-middle-class (e.g., Columbine) school districts. No school is immune to being affected by violence, and students are capable of perpetrating violence anywhere, under the right circumstances and given the right opportunity.

When do homicides and suicides occur at school? In an interesting study of homicides and suicides that occur during the school year, the CDC found that rates of school-associated suicides remain relatively stable over the school year.[4] Despite a great deal of evidence that rates of suicide in the general population occur more frequently during the spring and around specific holidays, there appeared to be no dramatic difference across months of the school year regarding risk for student suicides. Rates were slightly higher in the spring than in the fall, but there were no appreciable spikes in rates when examined across months of the school year, adjusting for the number of school days during that particular month (e.g., December had fewer school days due to the holiday vacation). What is important for schools to recognize is the increased risk among youth after one of their friends commits suicide during the school year. This clustering of suicides is a common event, and other vulnerable youth are at increased risk of suicide in the weeks immediately following the death of a friend or a popular student at school.

Unlike the trends for suicide, however, rates of homicide victimization at school were (1) much higher than the rates for suicide, (2) much less stable over time, and (3) spiked at very specific times during the school year. Which months during the school year are students most at risk for being the victim of a homicide at school? September and February. In fact, the lowest rates occurred in the late spring, during the months of May and June. What is going on during the months of September and February that makes them such high risks for serious violence? September is easier to explain. We know clinically that children who are having difficulty at school, whether it is academic difficulty, problems with peers, having trouble getting along with teachers, or just getting into trouble for their behavior, find the transition times at the beginning and end of school years to be the most problematic. Students who find school emotionally stressful have difficulty beginning the new school year with a new teacher, new peer group, and a different set of expectations for learning and performance. Emotionally or behaviorally fragile children may have difficulty transitioning from the relatively unstructured summertime setting, in which few expectations may be placed on them, to the more highly structured, demanding school schedule. They dread the unknown, experience anxiety about not being able to meet expectations, worry about the daily homework, and stress over grades.

Another big factor at the beginning of the school year is the level of disorganization and anonymity present in most schools. Teachers do not yet know all of the students in their classroom. If you are an older student, you no longer have just one main teacher but many teachers for multiple subjects, with different peer groups in every classroom. This makes it harder for students to feel engaged and harder for teachers to get to know the students. Many vulnerable children feel anonymous, left out, and uncared for. Who gets the attention at the beginning of the school year? The popular kids, the kids who are high achievers, and the troublemakers. Children who just fit in and don't stand out in any particular way can be left out, or can at least feel like they are being left out. It is not the actively rejected child that we should always be concerned about. The child who is always getting into trouble, fighting with other kids, or not getting along with teachers—this is the child that everyone knows about. The rejected child is the one your child describes when he gets home at night: "Johnny got into trouble again today at school. No one likes him." The kids know Johnny, and all the teachers know Johnny. If Johnny needs help, he's going to get it. If Johnny is too disruptive and needs intervention, he's going to get it.

What happens to Bobby, the average kid? His grades are OK. He comes to school every day and rarely misses without an excuse. He never gets into trouble or fights with the other kids. He probably doesn't belong to any particular peer group. He's not with the jocks; he's not with the nerds; he's not even with the vegans or the Goths. But maybe he's lonely and depressed. Maybe he's anxious about not fitting in. Maybe he's worried about being bullied out of his lunch money or his homework, or about being threatened to let someone else cheat off of him. Maybe he's angry about not being part of one of those peer groups, about not being popular because he just doesn't fit in. What do we do with Bobby?

Several things have struck me about the highly publicized school shootings over the past decade. First, with only one or two exceptions, they have all been male perpetrators. Second, none have occurred in urban schools, but many have occurred in middle-class and upper-middle-class suburban and rural settings, places many adults have believed were immune to the effects of severe violence. Third, and perhaps most distressing,

125

is the relatively common reaction among peers and teachers that goes something like this: "I never would have expected it to be him." The perpetrators of these horrible events have not been the students that others would have predicted could or would carry out such an act. These incidents have reinforced at least two phenomena about violent behavior among children and adolescents: (1) violence is a complex phenomenon, not easily understood and particularly not easy to predict, and (2) violence can happen anywhere, under the right circumstances and given the right opportunities.

The U.S. Secret Service and the U.S. Department of Education jointly completed a thorough study of the thinking, planning, and other preattack behaviors carried out by juveniles who committed school shootings from 1974 through 2000. Their report on the Safe Schools Initiative is available online at www.secretservice.gov/ntac. The ten key findings of the initiative are summarized below:

- Incidents of targeted violence at school rarely were sudden, impulsive acts.

- Prior to most incidents, other people knew about the attacker's idea and/or plan to attack.

- Most attackers did not threaten their targets directly prior to advancing the attack.

- There is no accurate or useful profile of students who engaged in targeted school violence.

- Most attackers engaged in some behavior prior to the incident that caused others concern or indicated a need for help.

- Most attackers had difficulty coping with significant losses or personal failures. Moreover, many had considered or attempted suicide.

- Most attackers felt bullied, persecuted, or injured by others prior to the attack.

- Most attackers had access to and had used weapons prior to the attack.

- In many cases, other students were involved in some capacity.

- Despite prompt law enforcement responses, most shooting incidents were stopped by means other than law enforcement intervention.

When Are Police Called to School?

Some schools have employed police officers or armed security guards as a way to enhance perceived security, deter crime, and provide a quicker on-site response to incidents of violence. While there is no consistent evidence that having police monitor hallways and lunchrooms results in a significant reduction in rates of crime and violence in a school (officers cannot possibly cover an entire school, so students intent on fighting, vandalism, or stealing will find a way to perpetrate their act away from the officer), police are often called to schools to intervene in a number of potentially violent circumstances. In the course of our work at the institute, we have had the privilege of working with the division of police in several communities and have had access to information regarding calls for service from local public schools.

First of all, it is important to note that police are called most often to middle schools, followed by elementary schools, and then high schools. When are they called most frequently? Our data, which consists of nearly 2,000 incidents from over seventy schools across a twenty-month period, suggests that police officers are most likely to be asked to respond to an incident at a school between the hours of 9 and 10 a.m. (right after school starts) and between 2 and 3 p.m. (right after older kids are dismissed). Elementary and middle schools experience higher levels of violence if they are located in close physical proximity to a high school. Rates of violent incidents after school decrease significantly if police officers are assigned to patrol the area around the high-risk schools between 2 and 4 p.m. Police patrols are particularly effective when an officer is accompanied by a school staff person the children know. These targeted patrols allow a consistent law enforcement presence in known high-risk schools at known high-risk times, and they also allow officers and school personnel a chance to establish meaningful working relationships with each other. As they get to know the children, the youth become less likely to engage in offending behavior and more likely to report offenses or potential fights to the members of the school-police team.

What types of incidents are police officers responding to? According to our data, the most frequent reason to call police officers to a school is assaults, which occur nearly 24 percent of the time. This is followed by altercations/fights (16 percent) and trespassing (11 percent). Threats and incidents with weapons make up nearly 8 percent and 5 percent of all incidents, respectively.

Bullying and Victimization from Violence at School

Bullying happens at every type of school. It knows no geographic, ethnic, or socioeconomic boundaries. Bullying affects children from elementary school through high school, and it seems to be particularly problematic during the middle school years, when being popular and belonging to a group are of the utmost concern to most youth. If bullying is so normal and expectable, why should we take it seriously? The first answer is that bullying and threatening behavior must be taken seriously because they often precede more serious acts of violence. Some studies estimate that 70 to 90 percent of youth will experience ongoing psychological or physical harassment at some point during their school years, characterized by exposure to bullying or being threatened with violence at school. About one in three youth will self-report that they have been often or frequently involved in bullying as the perpetrator, as the one who was bullied, or both. In one study, 8 percent of students reported being bullied one or more times per week, with an average of one bullying incident occurring at school every seven and a half minutes.

The second answer is that studies of bullying and child victimization from violence at school have shown that repeat victimization can significantly damage a student's emotional and social development. Being bullied is associated with low self-esteem, depression, social anxiety, and staying away from school (e.g., school avoidance).[5] About 8 percent of children report that bullying affects their lives so much that they have attempted suicide, run away, or refused to go to school, and 17 percent report suffering from academic problems due to bullying. Across three national Youth Risk Behavior Surveys, a measure developed by the federal CDC to assess rates of adolescent health compromising behaviors and violence, approximately

4 to 5 percent of high school students reported staying home at least one time in the past month because of safety concerns at or on the way to school. In other studies, 14 percent of high school students and 22 percent of fourth through eighth graders reported that bullying and school violence diminished their ability to learn in school. It is hard to concentrate on school when children are constantly worrying about the next time they will be harassed, what they can do to get revenge on their tormentor, or if they will become the next victim. Bullying is a common occurrence in our school's hallways, lunchrooms, restrooms, and playgrounds. It's not always physical fighting, but bullying can occur via verbal threats, name calling, emotional or sexual harassment, extortion of lunch money, or manipulation to make students share their homework or let another student cheat off them on a test. Bullying can be one individual against another individual, or it can be groups of youth victimizing another group or individual.

Who is doing the bullying? Males are more likely to be both the perpetrators and the targets of overt bullying, which occurs most frequently in middle school. Children who bully other children are more likely to come from homes that depend on the use of physical punishment, the assertion of power, and coercion as the model for punishment, discipline, and generally how members of the household interact with each other. This interpersonal style tends to be adopted by the child in his interactions with others, particularly with peers, but also with other adults. A bully is more likely to have parents who are not very warm or involved in their child's life. They are more likely to come across as disinterested, becoming engaged only when a crisis comes about. The parents of a bully are likely to be reinforcing the child's aggressive, coercive behavior. Finally, bullies typically lack much empathy for others and may themselves have poor self-concepts or poor self-esteem.

Who are the victims? The victims of bullies tend to be physically weaker or smaller than the aggressors. They are more likely to experience anxiety and to be passive and insecure in their interactions with others. Victims of bullies tend to be loners who lack some of the social defense skills you need to avoid getting into situations that increase the possibility of being victimized by a bully. Like bullies, victims often suffer from poor self-esteem, but for them this is related to their victimization status, not the overall lack of self-esteem that leads the bully to feel like he needs to dominate and control others to feel good about himself.

What happens to bullies and their victims? A great deal of research has been done on this topic in the past few years, particularly given the media reports that bullying played a role in making several of the school shooters feel alienated from their peers. Bullies are six times more likely to be convicted of a crime by the age of twenty-four and five times more likely to have a serious criminal record by the age of thirty. Bullies complete less schooling and are more likely to drop out of school then their peers, and if they are employed as adults, they end up in lower-status and lower-paying jobs. Victims of bullies don't fare too well either, especially if they are victims of chronic harassment and bullying over many years by many different perpetrators.

Victims of persistent bullying are at increased risk of eventually becoming more aggressive and violent themselves. A great deal of research has documented the association between victimization from violence and increased risk for perpetrating aggressive, violent behavior against others. In fact, there exists a cohort of youth who report being both bully and victim (about 6.3 percent of middle school students in one recent large school-based survey). Victims of bullying are also more likely to develop significant mental health problems such as depression and anxiety, and they report feeling socially isolated, without a way to cope with their victimization and without the social support they need to get out of the cycle of being bullied. Finally, victims of bullies also suffer academically. Many victims will stay home from school for extended periods of time just so they can avoid the bully. The longer the bullying goes on, the harder it is for the victim to recover from its effect on them socially, emotionally, and academically.

How do we stop the bullying? There aren't any quick or simple solutions to the problem of bullying, but there do exist some well-developed and widely implemented school-based bullying prevention programs.[6] Programs involve strategies like giving bullies special responsibility in the classroom, a move that has been shown to reduce child aggressive behavior, or making bullies responsible for the protection of possible victims. There is a focus on working with victims, teaching them strategies to avoid situations that increase the risk that bullying will occur, as well as developing the social skills that help them act assertively and confidently in situations with more aggressive peers. At a basic level, it means working with the victim to help them to ignore bullies, to walk away when it appears a bully is approaching them to instigate conflict, to tell the bully to stop loudly and assertively, and to immediately tell an adult if he is being hurt by someone else, either physically or emotionally.

It is also important to work with victims to develop their support network of peers and adults. They need their peers to help recognize potentially troublesome situations, to back them up when they try to avoid getting into a fight, or to stand up for them when they are being picked on by a bully. Adults are responsible for intervening quickly when they observe any instances of bullying going on in the hallways, on the playground, or on the school bus. Adults should also take responsibility for monitoring the hot spots in the school where bullying is most likely to occur (lunchrooms, restrooms, etc.), even if the monitoring does not fall under their specific job description. Lastly, programs work with bullies, victims, and adults to develop appropriate coping strategies with respect to intolerance, respect for others, effective problem solving, anger management, and mental health and well-being.

Threats and Violence

One type of bullying and victimization is when one child threatens to hurt another child. This is a form of interpersonal violence. When the school shootings were starting to show up in the national media, there was a great deal of discussion about the role of threats and whether threats were to be considered part of normal adolescent bantering or whether they should be take seriously every time they occur. Some of my colleagues appeared on national news shows stating that no data existed showing that kids who made threats were any more likely to hurt other kids than those who did not make threats. The reaction by school administrators across the country to each of the school shootings was expectable: zero tolerance for threats of any kind. The national news was replete with stories of youth expelled from school for making seemingly innocent comments that were perceived by someone else (another student or teacher) as a threat. One child was expelled because he wrote about "dying with honor" in an essay as part of a school assignment. Other reactions were clearly necessary, and some youth were suspended or expelled for very legitimate concerns. It is not normal to write up a hit list with student names and to diagram the school, marking spots where one intends to place explosive devices.

131

Students who openly discussed copycat incidents were identified to authorities. Hotlines for tips were put into place in many schools (although these are rarely used by callers to identify threats of violence).

But what about the rest of the students in a school who threaten to hurt other kids or teachers? Is this a normal feature of adolescent development that we should just tolerate, or should these threats be taken seriously? If a child makes a threat to hurt someone else, is he bound to do something about it, or is he just kidding? Is he just trying to intimidate someone, or will he eventually try to hurt someone else? These are all important questions that deserve serious consideration.

In our own work surveying children and adolescents about their exposure to violence, their mental health, and their aggressive, violent behavior, we asked them about whether they had ever made threats to hurt other students. We were interested in the association between making threats and the actual use of aggressive, violent behavior. We separated the sample into three groups: (1) those who never made threats to hurt anyone else (the nonthreateners), (2) those who admitted to threatening to hurt others once in awhile or rarely (infrequent threateners), and (3) those who admitted that they frequently threatened to hurt others (frequent threateners). This data comes from a sample of over 10,000 children and adolescents, in grades three through twelve, from three states, and who came from urban, suburban, and rural schools. Figure 7.1 illustrates what we found.

The bar represents the likelihood that an infrequent threatener will actually engage in the different types of violent behavior as compared to nonthreateners (the reference group, or the group at zero). Across all types of aggressive, violent behavior, infrequent threateners were about four to five times more likely to engage in that behavior than were children who did not threaten to hurt others. What about the frequent threateners? These youth were significantly more likely to engage in all forms of violence compared to both the infrequent threateners and the nonthreateners. Their relative risk ranged from being about eight or nine times more likely to hit someone else after being hit (compared to nonthreateners) to being more than twenty times more likely than a nonthreatener to attack someone else with a knife.[7] The data clearly show that children who admit to making threats to hurt other children are much more likely to also act in an aggressive, violent way compared to children who rarely make threats and to nonthreateners.

132

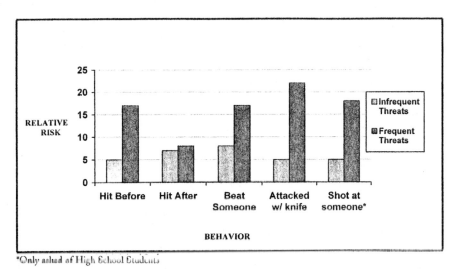

*Only asked of High School Students

Figure 7.1. Risk for Violent Behavior: Threateners vs. Non-Threateners

Are there any policy or practice implications of this finding? When a child or adolescent threatens to hurt another person, that threat needs to be taken seriously, and if other risk factors are present, that child should be assessed for violence potential. These other risk factors would include such things as a history of aggressive or violent behavior, high rates of exposure to violence or victimization, and mental health problems. Almost everyone recognizes the potential danger when a child makes statements to someone else that they are thinking about killing themselves. We have done a pretty good job of socializing professionals, adults, and even children about the need to take these threats of self-injury seriously and to tell someone else if we hear a child say something like that. We have well-developed clinical assessment protocols for determining the level of risk of suicide, and these help us plan a course of action and make recommendations. We have no such systematic protocol in place when children make threats to harm others. It is possible to prevent others from being harmed if a student who knows about a threat reports it to a responsible adult. There have been many incidents of violence that have been averted because a young person told someone else about a threat or plan for violence or that they heard someone had a hit list. In collaboration with the U.S. Secret Service, the U.S. Department of Education has compiled a nice, thorough, and easy-to-read guide on how to manage threatening situations and how to create safe school climates (available online at www.ed.gov/pubs/edpubs.html).

What about teachers? What role do they play in identifying children who make threats to hurt others? We were able to look at teacher reports of children who make threats and compare them to student self-reports of threatening behavior. This is an important question because we largely depend on teachers to tell us who the problem children are in their classroom. We depend on teachers to identify youth who are in need of additional assessment or services. We depend on teachers to pick out children who are different, who do not seem to be getting along well with their peers, or who seem to behave or perform academically in developmentally inappropriate ways.

When we tried to match teacher and student reports of who makes threats, we found that, as expected, the largest group of youth identified were students who self-reported that they never made threats to hurt others, and their teacher also reported they were nonthreateners (59 percent of the entire sample agreed on this point). The next highest group was made up of children who admitted to making threats but whom teachers reported were nonthreateners (23 percent), followed by students whose teachers reported that they made threats but who denied being a threatener (10 percent). The smallest group consisted of the match between teachers and students, where both reported that the student made threats to hurt others (8 percent). Children in the last two groups (18 percent) are most likely to be known by schoolteachers and administrators. However, nearly one in four children admit to making threats to hurt others (about half of them admit to frequently making threats to hurt others), and teachers don't know it! This can be a potentially serious problem for schools, but it also means that we should continue to work with young people (who are more likely to know who the threateners are) to report to adults when they know that one of their peers has made a threat to hurt someone else, so that appropriate and reasonable action can be taken. Where do bullies fall on this continuum? When examining teacher reports of child threats and violent behavior, bullies are over three hundred times more likely to be identified by teachers as frequently making threats to hurt others compared to nonthreateners.

Violence at School and Child Mental Health

In our own work, we find that between 5 percent (females reporting being beaten up) and 55 percent (males reporting being threatened at school) of children in elementary and middle schools, located in urban, suburban, and rural neighborhoods, report that they have been a *victim* of threats or hits or have been beaten up at school during the past year.[8]

Rates of child-reported witnessing of violence are higher than actual rates of victimization. We have found high rates of witnessing violence at school. Among adolescents, we found that an average of 29 percent (combined rates for males and females) reported seeing someone else beaten up at school in the past year, but a whopping 89 percent had witnessed someone else being threatened at school. Among elementary school students in grades three through eight, we found that 55 to 80 percent of children reported witnessing violent incidents at school within the past year. As the data in table 7.1 illustrate, younger children are also victimized by violence at school at much higher rates than are older youth.

In our surveys of adolescents, we found that youth exposed to high levels of violence at school, regardless of the amount of violent behavior they engaged in, were significantly more likely to experience higher levels of anxiety than were students who reported low levels of violence exposure at school. Students who are anxious and feel unsafe in their surrounding environment are less likely to be able to pay attention in the classroom, are

Table 7.1. Percentage of Students Who Report Being "Beaten up" at Home, School, and in the Neighborhood

Locale	Elementary School (grades 3–5)			Middle School (grades 6–8)			High School (grades 9–12)	
	Rural	Small City	Urban	Rural	Small City	Urban	Small City	Urban
Males								
School	23.9	19.7	17.6	8.3	9.6	11.3	5.4	9.8
Home	20.9	26.3	24.5	12.2	12.1	7.2	6.4	6.7
Neighborhood	18.2	27.8	20.9	7.2	8.0	13.4	11.5	16.4
Females								
School	8.9	7.6	12.4	1.4	4.3	8.9	4.0	4.4
Home	16.8	15.8	17.9	6.3	8.7	9.6	9.1	9.2
Neighborhood	4.4	17.2	12.7	1.4	2.2	10.0	3.8	7.0

Source: Flannery, D. (1997). School violence: Risk, preventive intervention and policy. ERIC Clearinghouse on Urban Education, Urban Diversity Series No. 109. Institute for Urban and Minority Education, Columbia University.

less likely to report that they enjoy going to school, and are overall less likely to be engaged in and attached to school. All of these factors have been associated with an increased risk of poor academic achievement and of engaging in problem behavior.

Adolescents who are exposed to violence at school also report being significantly more likely to engage in violent behavior, to bring a weapon to school, and to miss a significant number of days of school. Violence exposure has been linked to an increased risk for engaging in self-destructive and aggressive behavior. As we have previously discussed, students who are aggressive, delinquent, or violent are at increased risk for truancy, dropping out of school, and academic failure.

Whether a witness to or a victim of violence, exposure to violence is related to a number of emotional problems, such as post-traumatic stress, anxiety, anger, depression, and dissociation (these associations are discussed in greater detail in chapter 8). Specifically, children who are persistently victimized from violence suffer from higher levels of depression, anxiety, and loneliness compared to nonvictimized children. If left unattended in any form, violent behavior such as bullying can result in severe psychological, academic, or physical harm to the victim, irreparable harm to the perpetrator, and rejection of responsibility by the bystander/observer.

Along with a significant relationship to mental health, exposure to violence has been found to be positively associated with violent behavior and aggression. For example, in a longitudinal study, adolescent victims of child maltreatment prior to age twelve were 24 percent more likely to report violent behavior in high school than were nonviolent peers.[9] The effects of violence exposure on inner-city high school students has also been shown to predict hostility in adolescence.[10] Finally, adolescents who reported attacking another person with a knife or shooting at someone were significantly more likely to be exposed to violence than were youth who did not report these seriously violent behaviors.[11]

School Climate

Effective schools can exert a positive influence on student behavior and achievement despite conditions in the home, socioeconomic status, delinquent behavior, or other risk factors. In the past, it has been argued that schools cannot make a difference or overcome deficits, such as poverty, or help a child overcome multiple risk factors. However, more recent research has shown that some high-achieving schools are located in some extremely economically depressed urban neighborhoods. Level of academic achievement can also vary from school to school, regardless of community or neighborhood characteristics. School climate is one factor that has recently been implicated in student academic achievement and school success.

The climate of a school helps to shape the interactions between students, teachers, administrators, parents, and the community. School climate consists of the attitudes, beliefs, values, and norms that underlie the instructional practices, level of academic achievement, and the operation of the school. Some researchers have suggested that the lack of an orderly classroom environment and a lack of a sense of safety are major ingredients of a negative school climate. Students who do not feel safe and who believe they are in a highly disorganized place where adults have little interest in their well-being are more likely to suffer academically, socially, and emotionally compared to students who rate their school more positively with respect to climate.

Perceptions of danger at school are also likely to have a negative influence on a student's ability to pay attention or learn. If students fear for their safety, they are less able to focus on education and learning, and they instead begin to focus on their protection and well-being. Along with violence coming from other students and individuals within the school, violence can also come from the school. This violence is called systemic violence.

Systemic violence is defined as any institutional practice or procedure that adversely impacts individuals or groups by burdening them psychologically, mentally, culturally, spiritually, economically, or physically. Applied to education, systemic violence refers to practices and procedures that prevent students from learning, resulting in harm to the students. Examples of systemic violence include exclusionary practices that prevent specific students from engaging or participating in various school activities, clubs, or organizations. An overly competitive learning environment can be considered a form of systemic violence, for example, which in turn creates a negative school climate, one in which students are competing against each other for grades, attention, and rewards.

The toleration of abuse is another form of systemic violence in a school. If teachers and school personnel do not intervene when bullying, threats, or violence occur, students might begin to think that these behaviors are condoned or are at least not taken seriously at their school. This can increase behavior problems, delinquency, and exposure to violence, significant risk factors for academic failure. Unmonitored areas on school grounds are places where students can be exposed to violence or be victimized by violence. Often these are physical locations that teachers and administrators claim are not part of their responsibilities (e.g., restrooms), so supervision of these areas is lax. Transition times, like class changes, and locations where more disorganized behavior occurs (e.g., lunchrooms, playgrounds) also contribute to higher rates of disruptive and inappropriate behavior.

A school's disciplinary policies can also contribute to a culture of systemic violence, especially if those policies are rooted in principles of exclusion and punishment. When students are consistently punished, suspended, or expelled based on who they are (e.g., those perceived to be at risk for violent behavior or delinquency), they may start to have negative attitudes or aversive feelings toward school, ultimately becoming distanced from school, activities, and education. Other aspects of a school that influence school climate include the learning curriculum and standards, expectations of teachers in regard to mastery and achievement, and student attitudes and commitment to education. Schools have an obligation to create a safe environment for everyone, and school security should be a core task, developed to the point where professional standards and evaluation criteria can be applied to determine effectiveness and outcomes.

There are at least five required elements schools need to achieve a positive climate.[12] The first requirement is a safe environment where students and teachers can focus on academic and social skills development instead of worrying about personal safety. The second is a sequenced curriculum that is understood and supported by teachers and students and that also demands a high level of mastery from all students. Thus, students should only receive credit for work that demonstrates competence or that meets standards of performance. A third requirement is a commitment from the school administration and personnel to conduct ongoing assessments that reflect the goals and mission of the school. Such assessments would identify any weaknesses or limitations in the curriculum or educational plan that need to be redesigned, or any policies that are no longer serving the purpose of creating a positive school climate. Schools can conduct formal assessments of environment and safety via models like Crime Prevention Through Environmental Design (CPTED), available through organizations like the National Crime Prevention Council (NCPC).

The fourth requirement for a positive school climate is the elimination of school practices that are based on the assumption that many students cannot and will not be academically successful. Such policies include ability grouping or tracking, where some students are placed into low-achieving groups or tracks with low expectations for academic success. This strategy lowers child academic performance and behavior and can dramatically affect a student's academic self-concept and contribute to a sense of futility. The fifth necessary element to achieving a positive school climate is the affirmation and celebration of achievement for the purpose of enhancing student and teacher commitment to academic progress and to the mission of the school. A simple way schools can do this is by sponsoring and conducting awards programs so that students are recognized for their achievements. Overall, positive school climates exist when students have the opportunity to succeed and be rewarded for their effort. This enhances student motivation and achievement and has other positive school outcomes.

CHAPTER EIGHT
VIOLENCE AND MENTAL HEALTH: TWO BIRDS OF A FEATHER

Exposure to violence, either as witness or victim, and mental health are inextricably linked. Studies have repeatedly demonstrated a strong association between the two, with higher levels of exposure associated with more significant mental health symptoms. Among the most commonly noted symptoms are increased depression, anxiety, anger, and dissociation or desensitization to the effects of violence. These findings hold even when you look at children in different geographic locations, such as urban communities compared to suburban or rural communities. The link between exposure to violence and mental health symptoms holds for boys and girls and for youth from different ethnic groups and different family situations (e.g., two-parent and single-parent families). Given that children and adolescents are exposed to increasing amounts of violence on a daily basis, this is a disturbing trend, and one that we need to pay attention to if we are going to help young people adapt to their changing environments and effectively cope with the world around them.

In our own studies of children and adolescents, we've asked youth in schools about their levels of exposure to violence (witnessing violence and being victimized by violence) and their levels of mental health symptoms. These were children who were attending school, although because these were anonymous surveys, we did not ask if they had been receiving treatment for any mental health problems like depression or ADHD. The important point is that we did not specifically survey youth who had already been identified as having significant behavior or mental health concerns.

Table 8.1 summarizes our data on mental health symptoms for youth in elementary school grades three through eight and for high school students, separately by gender. For each mental health symptom (in this case, symptoms related to post-traumatic stress disorder, discussed below), we broke the group up into youth who reported very low levels of exposure to violence at school and youth who reported extremely high (e.g., in the top 10 percent of the group) levels of exposure to violence. The percentages of youth reporting clinically significant levels of mental health symptoms are reflected in the columns. Rates of mental health problems are similar whether we examine school violence exposure specifically or violence exposure in other settings, including the neighborhood and at home.

Several important themes emerge when we examine mental health symptoms as they related to violence exposure. First, we consistently find a significant number of youth in the high-exposure group reporting clinically significant levels of mental health symptoms, which means they are high enough that we would recommend they see a professional to assess whether they need further assistance or therapy. Second, the number of youth reporting serious mental health problems is actually higher for students in elementary grades than it is for adolescents. This is striking in that we always depict adolescence as the developmental period when

Table 8.1. Percent Clinical Range of PTSD Symptoms by Level of School Violence

Grades 3–8	Females		Males	
PTSD Symptom	Low	High	Low	High
Anger	2.9	14.3	1.4	16.3
Anxiety	4.6	23.2	2.2	14.7
Depression	4.6	20.1	3.3	17.6
Dissociation	4.6	19.6	2.5	15.7
Stress	4.3	18.7	2.2	13.5
Grades 9–12	Females		Males	
PTSD Symptom	Low	High	Low	High
Anger	2.5	13.1	5.7	33.3
Anxiety	3	13.3	1.2	9.8
Depression	3.2	11.7	3.3	11.7
Dissociation	2.9	10.5	2.1	8.9
Stress	1.5	11.9	3.3	12.3

Source: Flannery, D. (1997). *School Violence: Risk Preventative Intervention and Policy.* Monograph for the Institute of Urban and Minority Education, Columbia University and the Eric Clearinghouse.

youth, especially girls, are most likely to experience significant problems with mental health issues.

This latter phenomenon has been illustrated by my colleague James Garbarino in his best-selling book *Lost Boys: Why Our Sons Turn Violent and How We Can Save Them*.[1] There is no doubt that boys in the high-violence-exposure group report significantly higher levels of anger than do girls. One-third of adolescent boys in the high-exposure group report clinically significant levels of anger. This is a serious behavior and mental health problem for these young men. But what about the girls? Do they struggle with anger as well, or are they confined to battling internalized feelings like depression and anxiety?

The evidence from general studies of mental health problems reported by adolescents is consistent: girls report struggling with depressed mood and anxiety, whereas boys tend to report more anger, acting-out behavior, and school problems. We were interested in this difference between boys and girls and wondered if these findings would hold up if we looked at youth who were exposed to high levels of violence or who reported perpetrating high levels of violent behavior. One pragmatic issue is that most of what we have done historically in the field of prevention and treatment related to violence has been based on data collected from boys. Almost all of the early long-term studies of aggression, delinquency, and violence tracked only boys, because the evidence was that boys were the angry, acting-out ones, while girls kept their emotions inside. Girls were not the trouble-makers that everyone pointed to in school. If they were depressed or anxious, at least they were quiet, and overall they still did pretty well academically at school.

About ten years ago, we began including girls in studies of aggression and violence. In part, this started with investigations of girls in gangs, as anthropologists and criminologists noticed girls becoming more actively involved in gang activity and crime. This developed into a more consistent appreciation of the need to understand aggression and violence among females. While the overall levels of these behaviors among girls was not as dramatic as it was for boys (aggression and crime continue to be largely a male-dominated phenomena), the increased rate for these behaviors among girls far outpaced any increase in violent behavior we were seeing for boys.

In order to examine the issue of aggressive behavior and mental health among violent boys and girls, we decided to take our sample of high school students and try to identify the most violent youth, by the adolescent's own self-report of behavior.[2] We started with what would constitute describing an adolescent as being dangerously violent and decided that if a young person, by his or her own admission, reported that he or she had attacked or stabbed someone with a knife or had shot at or shot someone else with a real gun within the past year, he or she could be described as dangerously violent (for a community sample of youth). Stabbing or shooting at someone is much more serious than getting into fights with others, for example. By this initial process, we identified 584 adolescents from an overall group of 3,140 (n = 18 percent) who met the criteria for engaging in dangerously violent behavior in the past year. Violent females were more likely to report stabbing someone (65 percent) than shooting at someone (25 percent), and nearly one in ten said they had used both a knife and a gun to perpetrate violence in the past year. Boys were more likely to use a gun (48 percent), followed by stabbing someone with a knife (31 percent), but one in five also reported doing both (21 percent).

Because we were interested in what kinds of violence these youth were exposed to and in their mental health status, we sought to compare them to a group of their peers who were very similar on some basic characteristics, especially the ones that have been found to be related to differences in violence exposure, violent behavior, and mental health. So, the next step was to match our dangerously violent youth to other kids who were very similar to them demographically but who did not report engaging in such dangerously violent behavior. We matched our groups on demographic factors that included child gender, age in years, ethnicity, geography of residence (urban, suburban, or small-city community), and family structure (two-parent vs. single-parent). All told, we were able to match on all these factors 484 dangerously violent youth with a nonviolent peer. Once we got the two matched groups, we set about looking at their violence exposure and mental health.

As expected, dangerously violent adolescents reported significantly higher levels of exposure to violence than did the nonviolent matched controls, and they were much more likely to report clinically significant levels of all psychological trauma symptoms, including increased levels of anxiety, anger, depression, dissociation, and post-traumatic stress symptoms. Consistent with other descriptions of violent adolescent males, we found that dangerously violent males were three times more likely to report clinically significant levels of anger than were nonviolent males. What we didn't expect, however, was the high levels of anger among dangerously violent females, who were significantly more angry (more than double) than even the most violent males. Coupled with extremely high levels of depression, anger also puts violent females at a high risk for suicide compared to violent males and nonviolent adolescents.

As illustrated in figure 8.1, nearly one in five dangerously violent females self-reported significant risk for wanting to hurt or kill themselves, which was three times higher than for nonviolent females and over four times higher than for violent males. These data on the relationship between violence and mental health are compelling for a couple of reasons. First, they come from a community sample of adolescents who regularly attend school, and information about violence and mental health symptoms comes from their own self-report, not the reports of parents, teachers, or official police data. That they report such high levels of exposure to violence, serious violent behavior perpetration, and clinically significant levels of mental health problems is a significant concern. Second, it is important to note that extreme levels of anger are not unique to violent adolescent males. In this sample, levels of anger were even higher for violent females. In conjunction with the high levels of depression reported by

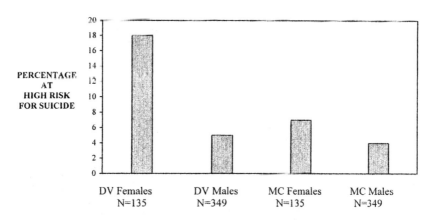

Note: DV = Dangerosly Violent; MC = Marched Controls

Figure 8.1. Self-Report of Wanting to Hurt or Kill Themselves

adolescent females, anger places them at an extremely high risk for suicide. Third, we compared groups of violent and nonviolent youth who were the same on a host of demographic factors usually associated with differences in violence exposure, violent behavior, and mental health problems. Our two groups were the same on all these characteristics, making us much more confident that the differences in mental health, for example, are due to differences between violent and nonviolent youth, not to differences due to gender, age, ethnicity, family structure, or where one lives geographically.

In fact, the way youth experience the effects of violence does not depend on where they live. How much (i.e., the level of) violence youth are exposed to (both as witness and as victim) does vary depending on where one lives, with youth in urban communities usually reporting higher levels of exposure than do youth in suburban or rural communities. Emerging research shows us that if children are exposed to violence, *regardless of the kind of community they live in or the type of school they attend*, they are at a high risk for experiencing significant mental health and behavior problems. In other words, a child in a rural community who is victimized by violence is just as likely to suffer from significant depression and anxiety as the inner-city youth who is bullied on his way to school and who also lives in a more violent neighborhood. Violence, when it occurs, impacts all youth in a significant way. It is not easier to take because children live in a nicer home or have nicer roads and rolling hills outside their door. The recent spate of multiple-homicide shootings at schools in this country highlights the danger of being complacent about violence and its impact on the mental health of young people. None of these dramatic shootings has occurred (yet) in an urban school setting. Very few of the perpetrators would have been identified by others prior to the event as youth at high risk of perpetrating such heinous acts of violence, and many who have acted out have been described as having significant mental health problems related to their violent behavior.

Multiple Homicides in Public Places

A few years ago, the *New York Times* ran a series of articles that examined all incidents of multiple homicides committed in public places since the early 1950s.[3] While the review was not conducted as a rigorous scientific study, the survey of rampage killings—where at least one person died in a public setting like a workplace, school, mall, restaurant, or on a train—was extremely thorough and informative. The series of stories identified one hundred cases of rampage killings that included twenty shootings at schools, eleven at restaurants or shopping malls, and thirty-two at the killer's workplace. Multiple killings that were the result of domestic violence, robbery, or political terrorism were not included in the study. In all, there were 102 perpetrators who killed 425 people and injured 510. Some of the information about the killers was gleaned from psychological autopsies of individuals after they had died, others from police reports of incidents and interviews with the suspects. What did they find?

1. There was little evidence that video games, movies, or television encouraged many of the attacks. In only six of the one hundred cases did the killers have a known interest in violent video games. Seven other killers showed an identifiable interest in violent videos.

2. There was usually a precipitating event that lead to the killing rampage. The most common precipitating event was job loss (forty-seven cases), followed by divorce or breakup of a relationship (twenty-two cases).

3. Threats of violence were made in most cases. Of the one hundred cases reviewed, sixty-three perpetrators had made threats of violence before the event, including fifty-four who had threatened specific violence to specific people. Thirty-five had a history of violent behavior and assaults. This is consistent with our findings of risk for perpetrating violence among children and adolescents generally, that those who threaten to hurt someone else are much more likely to act out in aggressive or violent ways compared to youth who do not make threats to hurt others.

4. There was a high incidence of capture and suicide. Unlike most perpetrators of violence and homicide, those who took part in rampage killings in public places either stayed at the scene of the crime until they were captured (eighty-nine

perpetrators never left the scene of the crime) or committed suicide. Thirty-three of 102 offenders killed themselves immediately after committing their crime (at the scene, so they are also included in the eighty-nine who did not flee), and four killed themselves later. Nine offenders were killed by police officers or others on the scene, perhaps committing what is often referred to as suicide by cop. This occurs in instances when an offender forces police officers or others to shoot at them as the way to end a confrontation. They point their weapon at officers, refuse to give up, or shoot at them, virtually forcing police to open fire, often killing the offender.

5. Teenage killers often obtained support from their peers and boasted of their plans to others. For example, on November 5, 1995, Jamie Rouse (seventeen years old at the time) walked down the hall of Richland School in rural Giles County, Tennessee, with a .22 Remington Viper. He shot two teachers and a student resulting in two deaths. He had told as many as five of his teenage friends exactly how he planned to bring his rifle to school and begin killing. One stated, "He told me something was going to happen at school the next day, and that I was going to lose a couple of friends." None of the friends told anyone or called anyone for help. Adults who committed rampage killings often acted alone, planning their crime on their own, although investigations have revealed that they also often broadcast their intentions, at least in general terms, to others.

6. More than half of the killers had histories of serious mental illness as evidenced by a previous hospitalization, a prescription for psychiatric medication, a suicide attempt, or psychosis (thought disorder). Does this prove the link between mental health and violence? One qualifier has to do with whether the previously identified mental illness was being treated. Of the twenty-four perpetrators on psychiatric medication at the time of the killings, fourteen had stopped taking the medication when they committed the crime. Larger studies have consistently shown that individuals with mental illness are no more violent than other people, except when

they are off their prescribed medications or have been abusing drugs or alcohol. One other note: in these rampage killings, when a mental illness was diagnosed via psychological autopsy (after the crime had been committed), the signs of mental deterioration or mental illness had sometimes been missed or dismissed by family members, teachers, colleagues at work, or even mental health professionals who had been working with the perpetrator.

The *New York Times* review of rampage killings provides several important pieces of information about the relationship between violence and mental health. While perpetrators of violence often have histories of mental illness, the likelihood that they will act in a violent way toward others is high only if they stop undergoing treatment (via drugs or therapy) or if they are abusing alcohol or are under the influence of some other drug. There is also some evidence that individuals with serious thought disorders (e.g., schizophrenia) coupled with paranoia are more likely to act out in a violent way in specific circumstances, like when they feel threatened. The problem of violence among individuals with mental illness is becoming more significant, however, as we limit accessibility and affordability of mental health and psychiatric services. Limited resources in some communities have also resulted in the release of mentally ill individuals from institutional settings, often putting them back on the streets without adequate support.

Post-Traumatic Stress Disorder

Post-traumatic stress disorder (PTSD) is a clinical term that first appeared as a psychiatric diagnosis in the early 1980s. In fact, PTSD has evolved over many years, mainly as we observed the impact of exposure to war and violence among members of the military. The severity, duration, and proximity of an individual's exposure to the traumatic event are the most important factors affecting the likelihood of developing the disorder. Community-based studies have shown a lifetime prevalence of PTSD ranging from 1 to 14 percent, while studies of at-risk populations (those who have already experienced trauma or who are likely to experience trauma) show prevalence rates as high as 60 percent.

Lenore Terr, who has studied the impact of trauma extensively among children, emphasizes four types of symptoms that most children who have experienced trauma typically display: (1) repeatedly perceiving memories of the event through visualization or "reseeing" aspects of the trauma; (2) engagement in behavioral reenactments and repetitive play related to aspects of the trauma; (3) trauma-specific fears; and (4) pessimistic attitudes about people, life, and future, manifesting as a sense of hopelessness and difficulty in forming close relationships. Terr also makes the useful distinction between traumas that result from "unanticipated single events" (type I trauma) and those that result from longstanding or repeated exposure to multiple events (type II trauma). While brief traumas may have only limited effects on the individual, repeated trauma may lead to anger, despair, profound psychic numbing, and dissociation, resulting in major personality changes (and impact on the brain).[4]

It is important to recognize that while the symptoms of PTSD can be very serious, most are normal and expectable for someone to go through after they have experienced trauma. For example, after one has gone through a traumatic experience, we would expect them to be somewhat more anxious, especially in similar situations or settings that bring back memories of the traumatic event. We would also expect someone to be more hypervigilant and hyperaroused, perhaps preparing themselves physically and emotionally for the possibility that they will reexperience the trauma and its related feelings (either in reality or through memories and associations). Finally, it would be normal to expect an individual to try to avoid the situations and settings that bring on the memories, feelings, and physical reactions related to the trauma and PTSD symptoms. Unfortunately, avoidance is often not possible for children to achieve, especially for those who find themselves being repeatedly exposed to violence in a setting such as their home where they cannot easily escape.

Suicide and Depression

Emotionally, adolescence is a time when most young people go through periods where they report feeling depressed, lonely, and perhaps even hopeless about their future. They spend a great deal of time thinking about how they fit in with others, about their identity, and about their relationships with peers (both same- and opposite-gender relationships). Some of the emotional roller-coaster ride can be attributed to the chemical changes occurring in the developing adolescent's brain, particularly because the hormones that are related to the physical changes of adolescence are also related to emotional changes. For example, studies of depressed adolescents who attempt suicide show that their brains have significantly lower levels of the hormone CSF 5-HIAA (the hormone serotonin). Part of the roller-coaster ride is related to the changes that are occurring in relationships with family and friends, and part of it can be traced back to individual personality traits or characteristics (remember the discussion on resilience and frustration tolerance, how flexible an individual is, etc.). Studies of adolescents who complete daily diaries show that most youth feel alone and sad at least some of the time, especially when they have not yet gotten to the point of being able to effectively use their available support systems (e.g., friends, family, school) and coping strategies when they feel stressed out. Almost all adolescents report having at least thought about suicide or what it would feel like to be dead, what the world would look like if they weren't around, or how one's friends or family would react if they died. Thinking about suicide and death is a normal part of growing up, and parents shouldn't be alarmed if their child asks questions about these things. Thinking about suicide and death in general is very different, however, from a depressed adolescent having thought through a specific and detailed plan to commit suicide.

Suicide continues its stronghold as the third leading cause of death for adolescents (after motor vehicle accidents and homicide).[5] The suicide rate among young people has been increasing steadily since the 1980s, and increases are not just confined to the United States. For example, in New Zealand, which has one of the highest youth suicide rates among developed countries, the suicide rate among persons fifteen to twenty-four years of age more than doubled from 1985 to 1995.[6] We've done a fairly good job of educating parents, teachers, and youth about the seriousness of statements about suicide. Any comment about suicide from a young person must be taken seriously and investigated to determine whether further action should be taken to help the child. Not all utterances are indicative of serious intent, but by the same token, not all jokes are really just jokes. Some are volleys over the bow of the ship that warn us of the seriousness of a young person's deteriorating mental health.

What separates comments about suicide from gestures, and gestures from serious attempts to complete the act? A couple of major contributing factors that should always be taken into account are any circumstances, events, or crises that may have occurred related to any comments about suicide. Adolescents who have just experienced a romantic breakup, the death (or suicide) of a friend or family member, a major fight with a parent, or some other major event are at increased risk for suicidal ideation or suicide. Another major factor is the young person's mental status. Youth who are depressed, anxious, or are expressing a sense of hopelessness or helplessness are more likely to attempt suicide than are youth who are not experiencing significant mood disorders or other psychiatric problems. A third major factor is previous suicide attempts, which is the most significant and reliable predictor of future attempts.

When I was a young psychology intern in Detroit, I spent a fair bit of time working in the emergency room of a local children's hospital. One of my responsibilities was to respond to incidents of suicide attempts. Over the course of a year, I never had occasion to interview a male who had attempted suicide. Scores of studies have shown that males are much more likely to use more lethal methods in completed suicides and suicide attempts compared to females. These methods include the use of firearms, hanging, jumping, and vehicle exhaust. Females, on the other hand, are more likely to use less lethal methods, particularly self-poisoning with medication or other drugs. In one recent study, over 60 percent of male suicides and serious suicide attempts involved the use of these highly lethal methods, whereas for females, 92 percent of all fatal and nonfatal serious suicide attempts involved less lethal methods, particularly self-poisoning with medication.[7]

When I would interview females in the emergency room, I would ask about the circumstances that lead up to the attempt, the method and plan they had used for the attempt, questions about their general mental health status, and a series of questions about their expectations for the future. When intervening in suicide-attempt situations at the hospital, there are basically three options for youth: (1) send them home and do nothing else; (2) send them home with their guardian and require that they see someone on an outpatient basis as soon as they are able; or (3) don't let them go home but hospitalize them until they are emotionally and medically stable and able to pursue additional treatment options. The first choice is rarely an option because few youth come into a hospital emergency room because they simply made a comment or gesture that has little basis for concern about safety or future risk. The second option may be preferred if the youth has no history of previous attempts, if there are no obvious serious mental health issues related to the event, if the gesture was impulsive and poorly thought out, if the youth has a strong support system of parents and medical care, and if both the youth and a guardian commit to seeking immediate medical and therapeutic help in an outpatient setting. The last option is reserved for those youth who have made a serious attempt and who are at imminent risk for hurting themselves or others. These youth may need constant supervision for a period of time to ensure that they will not attempt to hurt themselves again. Youth who have tried to hurt themselves before; who have made a serious, potentially lethal attempt that was well planned out; who appear to be in a constant state of crisis with little support available to them for coping (or few internal resources for coping effectively) are potentially good candidates for hospitalization or residential care. The safety and well-being of the youth is the ultimate criterion for whatever decision is made. Sometimes a clinician may feel that the most appropriate option is hospitalization, but changes in the health care industry regarding resources (e.g., insurance, bed availability) make this option increasingly more difficult to obtain for some youth and families.

The seriousness of the attempt is a significant consideration for treatment options. A young girl who has a fight with her boyfriend and responds by going home and emptying out the medicine cabinet, consuming vitamins, birth control pills, and cold medicine, is a different scenario and perhaps poses a different level of imminent risk than the girl who has tried to hurt herself before, who is significantly depressed, and who tried to kill herself by stockpiling lethal medications, waiting until she was alone in the house before pulling the phone plug, locking herself in the bathroom, and ingesting two bottles of her antidepressant medication and Ritalin with a bottle of vodka. I don't ever recall interviewing an adolescent female in the emergency room who said that she would try to hurt herself again if I let her go home (until I pointed out that they had tried to hurt themselves before). When asked, patients always agreed that if there had been a firearm easily available to them at the time of their attempt, they probably would have used it.

Youth suicide is a serious form of intrapersonal violence (violence against oneself) and is on the rise. We need to take this risk seriously and watch for the signs that a young person may be depressed or angry or feel hopeless about her future. Depression (and generally mood disorders) and recently experiencing stressful life events are two of the most significant risk factors for serious suicide attempts, along with previous attempts. A couple of cautionary notes are necessary about depression, however. Studies have shown that adolescents who make a serious suicide attempt are likely to be depressed (about 70 percent of the time), but those who complete suicide are much less likely to be described as recently depressed by those who know them well. One possible explanation is that youth who are serious about ending their life may feel more capable and motivated to act as their depression is lifting as opposed to while in the throes of depression, when energy level and motivation to act may be low. The message is that we should not be lulled into a false sense of recovery for adolescents who may seem to be doing better emotionally even though they have a significant history of serious suicide attempts. How many times have we heard the anguish of "He seemed to be doing better" soon after a young person takes his life?

The biological connection between the brain and suicide risk has also been studied. It may be that individuals at higher risk for suicide attempts are less able to control their impulsivity, especially if they also suffer from a mood disorder, or they may be less able to cope effectively with environmental and interpersonal stressors that often preclude a serious suicide attempt. The research that has been conducted on this link has shown, for example, that suicide attempts occur more often in depressed patients with low CSF 5-HIAA levels (low serotonin).[8] As we discussed earlier in the chapter on brain development, serotonin is most often associated with impulse control, with low levels of serotonin related to poorer control. Depressed patients with the lowest levels of serotonin have been shown to be much more likely to attempt suicide with violent methods like firearms or jumping compared to taking a harmful dose of medication.

One other caveat is worth mention. There is a phenomenon we call suicide clustering. This is the ripple effect of youth suicides, which reflects a spike in suicide attempts in the immediate aftermath (one to two weeks) of the suicide or death of a well-known or well-liked peer, or the suicide of an older sibling. There are many possible explanations for this phenomenon, but one that makes the most sense to me is that a vulnerable adolescent may view all of the attention, crying, and adulation that is bestowed upon a young person who dies and believe that she would receive the same outpouring of love, affection, and memorializing if she were to take her own life. This is not to say that we should avoid displays of grief and remembrance, because these are important coping strategies. Rather, we have to be careful about the potential of a ripple effect among other young people who may be particularly vulnerable during this emotionally stressful time. The bottom line is that if you have concerns about a young person's risk for suicide, the safest thing to do is to get them professional help as soon as possible. If it means taking the young person to the emergency room, so be it. Better here to be safe than sorry.

CHAPTER NINE

COPING MEANS DEALING WITH STRESS AND VIOLENCE ON A DAILY BASIS

The day was April 15, 1999. I won't ever forget it, not because it was a particularly bad tax day that year, but because that was the day we found out that our oldest son, Joseph, was diabetic. I remember driving home in the car thinking about our trip the next day to Santa Fe, New Mexico, when the cell phone rang. My wife was sobbing uncontrollably at the other end. My heart immediately began racing. What's wrong? Is everything OK? She had taken Joe to the pediatrician that day because a couple of weeks before he had inexplicably begun wetting the bed at night after being dry at night for years. He was five. "I'll just run him to the doctor to get him checked out before we leave," she had commented that morning. She and I were going to a conference together, the first trip we were going to take together without the kids since Joe was born. Although we had lived in Arizona, we had never made it over to visit Santa Fe, and we were both looking forward to our return to the southwest.

We thought Joe had a urinary tract infection or some other minor problem. Instead, our lives (and his) changed forever that day. Five minutes into his appointment, our pediatrician came back into the room and got teary eyed. My wife, completely taken aback, asked him what was wrong. "I think Joe has diabetes," he stammered. "You need to take him to the emergency room right away to have him checked out." My wife called me from the hospital. I started driving faster, feeling helpless that I was not there with them.

They tested Joe's blood sugar again in the emergency room. It was nearly 400. "Not a good sign," they said. "We need to admit him to find out what is going on," they said. So we admitted him, and we sat with him, not really telling him anything more than that he hadn't been feeling well and we needed to make sure he was OK before we went on our trip. We sat with him throughout the night, and they monitored his blood sugar every hour, even as he slept. By morning, he was down to normal. Maybe this was a temporary thing? Maybe he just had an infection or something? We hoped, and we even prayed a little.

Early the next morning, the endocrinologist from the hospital walked into Joe's room. "Oh no." she said, as she saw me standing there. "I noticed the name and hoped it wasn't you." We knew each other professionally. "I'm so sorry that we're seeing each other under these circumstances." (Another not-so-good sign, I thought). "Let's find out what's happening with Joe," she stated, loud enough for him to hear.

Joe came over, and the doctor said, "Joe, I want you to take this dollar and go down to the vending machine and pick out whatever candy you want and eat it. Then, after a little while, we'll test your blood sugar again and see what's up." This is known as challenging Joe (or at least challenging his system, because giving Joe money and telling him to go to the vending machine to pick out candy has never been a challenge for him, other than having to decide what to buy). To no one's surprise, Joe picked out the peanut M&M's, cheerily exclaiming, "Dad, I picked these out 'cause they're my favorite, and I know they're your favorite too." He even offered me a few, which I uncharacteristically refused: "You go ahead, Joe. They're all yours today. Go for it." Joe devoured his peanut M&M's in record time, smearing chocolate across his face, which bothered him not in the least.

They tested Joe's blood sugar again a little while later: 500. Joe was clearly diabetic. Telling Joe that he was diabetic and what that meant for him was one of the hardest things we've ever had to do as parents. But what came next is why this story is important to what it means to be resilient and cope with adversity. Because he was confirmed to be diabetic, we immediately began learning how to draw up insulin in syringes and began practicing giving injections to an orange, and eventually to each other (my wife and I). To think, just twenty-four hours earlier, we were set to be on our way to New Mexico. Life can change in an instant.

Later that morning, it was time to give Joe his first shot. My wife immediately turned to me and said, "You have to do this. I won't be able to do it for him without crying." Understandably, she left the room. It was me, Joe, and the nurse. She gave me the needle. "What are you going to do with that, Daddy?" Joe's eyes got wider, and the look of fear and anxiety quickened across his face. "I have to give you a shot, Joe, just like we talked about, OK?" I tried to be as gentle and reassuring as I knew how, fighting against the urge to just scream out loud how unfair it all was. I moved closer to Joe and gently grabbed his arm, pinching his skin as I prepared to stick him with the needle. "No, Daddy!" Joe screamed, loud enough for everyone on the floor to hear. He immediately began flailing his arms, kicking his legs, and screaming louder and louder. You know how strong kids can be when you're trying to get them to do something they really don't want to do? I could barely hold on to him. I literally had to lie on top of Joe and force him to the floor, holding him down so that I could give him his first shot. "You're hurting me. You're hurting me, Daddy! Why are you doing this to me? Mom, help me! Stop hurting me!" He was sobbing, pleading, begging for me to let him go. Of course, I couldn't. I gave him the shot and immediately picked him up off the ground. "I'm sorry, Joe. Daddy's sorry it hurt, but it's something we have to do so that you stay healthy," I tried to reassure him, to no avail.

The nurse left the room. My wife had fled down the hall when she heard the screams. I picked Joe up, hugged him, and put him on my lap in a rocking chair. I began rocking him back and forth slowly, trying to calm him down. After a minute or two, he began to breathe easier and curled up in my lap. As much as I didn't want to, I began to cry. A little bit at first, but that just led to a lot. I couldn't help it. Almost immediately, Joe stopped his own sniffling. He looked up, put his hand on my cheek, and turned my head so I was facing him.

"Don't cry, Daddy. It will be OK. We'll be OK." I didn't know what to say. Several moments of silence passed, and then he asked, "Would you like to be alone for a little while?"

"No, Joe, I just want to be with you," I replied. More seconds of silence.

"Do you want me to get you a Kleenex?" was the next thing to come from Joe, which made me burst out laughing. Here I had just held him down to give him his first shot, screaming, and now he was telling me that it would be OK! He was thinking about me, not about himself. Joe was trying to make me feel better. I was so proud of him that all I could do was hold him a little tighter and share a laugh in a moment that must have been many times more horrible for him than it was for me. I don't know how he was able to respond that way at five years old, and I don't know why he has been able to adapt to being diabetic, but his mom and I are sure glad he has pretty much been able to cope with diabetes and not let it dictate the things he does or tries on a day-to-day basis.

What does it really mean when we say that someone is coping well with a situation? Does it mean that he is putting on a smile even though we know he is experiencing extreme emotional stress over the recent death of a family member? Or does it mean that despite living with a whole bunch of crummy problems (financial disaster, poor health, relationships that always seem to be falling apart), he always seems to be in a good mood? Does it mean being resilient? How about having a high tolerance for frustration or pain or discomfort? What about just plain being able to get through the day without falling completely apart? It probably means a little bit of all of the above. Coping means being able to function on a daily basis despite facing adversity, crises, or chronic stressors. In clinical terms, coping refers to the ability to maintain a sense of equilibrium or balance in the face of crises.

Why is it that some children seem to be able to face adversity, continue to go with the flow, and adapt to even the most stressful and destructive circumstances, even when they appear to have very little going for them like a supportive family, financial means, or a good educational system? On the other hand, we all know children who come from good families, go to good schools, have many people who care for them, and who have all the material resources they could ever dream of having. Yet, as soon as they are faced with even the most seemingly minor frustration, stress, or challenge, they fall apart.

We call the first child resilient and the second child fragile. The term *resilience* refers to the ability to cope positively with adversity and stress. The resilient child is more likely to have an easy temperament, to be able to adapt well to new situations, and to persist in the face of frustration. He is more likely to continue working on a task even if it is challenging rather than give up out of anger or frustration. The first child is more likely to be a success seeker rather than a failure avoider, and he is more likely to seek out tasks that are challenging rather than those that are so easy that he is sure to be successful. Conversely, the failure avoider may seek out a task so hard that he is doomed to failure, thus giving him a reason for his lack of success (i.e., it was way too hard anyway).

Let's say you have two children who make their way to the neighborhood carnival. The resilient child, as a success seeker, is more likely to go to the ring-toss game and stand a few feet behind the table, making the task appropriately challenging. The fragile, failure-avoider child is more likely to either lean way over the table, almost assuring success, or to stand so far back that there is no way (other than sheer luck) that he will get a ring on the bottle. The resilient child is likely to pick challenging classes and tasks at school (like the books he chooses to read), whereas the easily frustrated child will pick books or tasks that are either extremely easy, guaranteeing success, or so difficult that he is sure to fail. More resilient children are more likely to ascribe success or failure on a task to their own effort (internalizing their success) rather than to luck or some other external factor beyond their control (e.g., it was too hard).

We don't know all the reasons why some children appear resilient and others do not, but we seem to know resilience and coping when we see it. Part of it is certainly genetics and temperament. Some children seem born with personalities that make them more resilient and able to adapt to challenges than other children. Part of it is environmental, because we know that it helps children to cope with stress when they have appropriate support systems in place when things get tough—no child is expected to deal with all things nasty on their own without help. Being a good problem solver and having effective parents, for example, appear to help children do better under conditions of severe adversity, and when these things are not present, children do much worse when crises arise. What is really striking about all of the research on what makes kids resilient is the seeming ordinariness of the phenomenon. In other words, being resilient appears to be much more common than most of us think. Being resilient reflects a basic human need to adapt; it serves as a survival mechanism— if we weren't resilient and didn't naturally seek to adapt to bad situations to make them better and to cope in the face of crises, then we would surely not survive as long or live to prosper and succeed. Many people eventually figure out how to get by, despite their circumstances and lot in life.

Research on Coping and Resilience

With respect to the research that has been done with children and adolescents, coping and being resilient includes such characteristics as being socially competent, having good problem-solving skills, being autonomous (independent), being able to maintain some control over one's emotions, having a sense that one's actions result in a consequence that one feels some responsibility for (self-efficacy), and having a sense of purpose and hopefulness about one's future. These individual characteristics are summarized in table 9.1.

Social Competence

Social competence is an area that is receiving increased attention in the field of prevention and intervention, particularly with respect to violence and mental health. A decade ago, much of our work was aimed at reducing the number and impact of various risk factors. If we reduced risk, we thought we could significantly affect whether a child would drop out of school, become delinquent or gang involved, or begin using drugs. What we forgot about (or at least paid little attention to) was the need to

Table 9.1. What It Means To Be Resilient

Construct	Description
Socially competent	Flexible; empathic; high frustration tolerance; effective communication skills; maintains a sense of humor; generally engages in prosocial behavior; gets along well with others; has the ability to meet expectations (e.g., at home, school)
Problem-solving skills	Capacity to think abstractly; fluency and flexibility of thinking; able to take the perspective of others, see another person's point of view.
Autonomy, self-efficacy	Capacity to exercise self-control (self-regulation); take initiative; take responsibility for one's actions and their consequences (not just having high self-esteem or positive self-concept)
Sense of purpose, hopefulness	Being hopeful about the future: goal-directed; success-seekers vs. failure avoiders; sense of achievement motivation (impact on school); persistent in the face of frustration and failure; focuses on effort as well as outcome

also increase those social skills and competencies that would allow children to adapt and make good decisions over the long term, improving their overall chances of success. It has not been until the past few years that the field has recognized that along with reducing risk we must also work to improve social skills and increase child competence. We see this in the increased emphasis in the field of education, for example, on character education and changing the climate of a school as opposed to merely focusing on individual child risk factors related to problem behavior, mental health, and academic achievement.

Problem Solving

Sometimes how we cope with things has as much do with opportunity and timing, especially the critical choices we make at different times in our lives, as it does with any internal resources we may possess to deal with stress (e.g., cognitive skills, temperament). Hanging out with friends who make bad choices and who put us in situations where bad things can happen more often is likely to affect our ability to cope with things and adapt to problem situations. If we haven't developed good problem-solving strategies and we are regularly in situations that require we make tough decisions (and we don't), then we are much more likely to end up at risk for problem-behavior outcomes compared to someone who has limited opportunities to get into trouble. When in trouble, at-risk youth also lack the capacity and support system to make positive decisions rather than choices that will get them into more trouble.

As parents, we all hope our children will grow up and make good decisions when they are faced with tough choices. We know that they might not always make the right choice, and certainly they won't always make the same choices we would make (if we only knew then what we know now), but we hope that we socialize them to become caring, responsible, and respectful adolescents and young adults who don't place themselves in bad situations or circumstances where there are no good choices and even fewer positive outcomes. One core aspect of good problem-solving skills has to do with the fluency and flexibility of our thinking. Fluency of thinking refers to the number of different possible solutions we are able to generate to any given problem or the number of different choices we are able to generate in response to a particular situation. You've probably heard about the one where you're asked a question like, "How many different things can you do with a brick?" The number of different possible answers you can come up with would generally reflect your fluency of thinking. Flexibility of thinking has to do with your ability to pick and choose an appropriate response to a particular problem, which is somewhat different from how many possible solutions you are able to generate. Being flexible in your thinking means you are pretty good at choosing an effective strategy to solve your problem, and if the first strategy doesn't work, you are flexible enough to move to the next best strategy and try that one.

Adolescents who find themselves frequently getting into trouble, making bad choices, and hanging out with the wrong crowd are probably not very fluid or flexible in their thinking. Of course, some adolescents are very quick on their feet, able to generate lots of solutions to problems, but they just tend to select what we would consider to be inappropriate solutions or strategies, or things that are generally against the law or would hurt other people. Some antisocial or conduct-disordered youth are very bright and capable of generating lots of possible responses, but because they lack empathy, are narcissistic, or are full of anger and frustration, their fluency and flexibility of thinking gets lost in the poor decisions and outcomes they pursue.

Autonomy and Self-Efficacy

Achieving a sense of autonomy and independence is one of the hallmarks of development. We see it in the push-pull of toddlerhood as children go off to explore their environment, only to look back furtively over their shoulder to make sure that Mom or Dad is still there watching over them. We see it in elementary grades, when children who are so excited about going to school on their own and learning are also afraid to ride the bus by themselves for the first time. We certainly see it in adolescence, when much of the conflict youth experience with parents has to do with an adolescent's striving for independence and autonomy at the seeming expense of parental influence, monitoring, and closeness.

Self-efficacy is another concept important for healthy development and must be distinguished from self-concept and the ever-present emphasis on self-esteem. Efficacy is the sense of responsibility and connection a person feels between his actions and the outcomes associated with those actions. To be efficacious means that you believe that what you do and how you behave will matter, that you can have an impact on what happens to you and to others. It also means that you are likely to take responsibility for your actions and that you believe you can change a negative outcome to a more positive one because you have some control over what happens to you. Having a sense of self-efficacy means that your life is not run by chance, luck, or happenstance.

Efficacy is very different from self-concept and self-esteem. Self-concept is how we perceive ourselves in our roles: I am a father, I am a teacher, I am a brother, or I am a cook. Self-esteem is the value label we place on our self-concepts: I am a good father, I am a supportive brother, I am a poor cook. We used to think that improving a child's self esteem, making him feel better, was all that really mattered. Self-esteem-promoting programs were all the rage in schools ten or twenty years ago, and the message was clear: just make kids feel better about themselves, no matter what. We forgot to attach consequences to behavior, responsibility to action, and outcomes to effort. We began praising kids regardless of their performance, effort, or behavior: "It's OK, Johnny, you're important no matter what you just did." While the underlying tone of the message is important to keep in mind, that all children have value and importance and that no one is perfect, we began to placate our children and inadvertently excused their behavior and performance. Over time, we realized that having high self-esteem was no buffer to problem outcomes. Violent offenders, for example, often have a very high sense of self-esteem; they feel pretty good about themselves and what they do or have done. For healthy development, coping, and adaptation, the focus should be on developing a healthy sense of efficacy and a sense of being responsible for one's actions, not merely having high self-esteem regardless of one's behavior or the consequences of one's actions.

Hopelessness

Youth who lack a sense of hopefulness about their future are at significant risk for behavior and mental health problems. They are much more likely to perpetrate violence against others and to lack any sense of empathy, remorse, or responsibility for their actions. Individuals who persistently dwell on the past will not be able to effectively cope with what is happening in the present and will not develop the capacities and competencies to deal effectively with challenges and crises that will occur in the future. Some at-risk youth don't believe that they will live very long and expect to die in their early twenties (or at least to be incarcerated by then). For youth who lack any sense of having a future, it is difficult for them to care very much about the long-term consequences of any of their decisions or actions. They are much more likely to live in the moment, to react to things impulsively, and to only be concerned with how a particular situation or problem affects them in the immediate future. There may be no tomorrow, let alone ten years from now.

How Do Adolescents Cope with Stress and Violence?

In our own work examining violence and mental health among adolescents,[1] we became interested in how adolescents who lived in high-violence environments coped with the daily stress of witnessing violence and being victimized by violence. Not only were we interested generally in how youth reported coping with these stressors, but we were also interested in finding out more about the coping strategies and mental health problems of youth who reported engaging in high levels of aggressive or violent behavior. We thought that the most violent youth would be more likely to report using inappropriate or maladaptive coping strategies compared to less aggressive youth. To get the most violent youth, we ranked the entire group on self-reported aggressive and violent behavior and took those in the top 10 percent as the most violent. Table 9.2 compares the percentage of youth who endorsed a variety of coping strategies (they could choose more than one) they used when they were upset. The percentages are broken down by violent and nonviolent youth and by gender. The sample included over 3,700 adolescents in grades nine through twelve in urban, suburban, and rural high schools.

A few things are striking about these percentages. The top two strategies, listening to music and talking to a friend, were the two most frequently endorsed coping strategies by all adolescents, regardless of whether they were violent or not, and this did not differ between males and females. The music youth reported listening to, by the way, was not mellow, soothing music. The second group of strategies were more often

Table 9.2. Percentage of Adolescents Using Each Coping Strategy at Least Sometimes

Coping Strategy	Most Violent Females N=191	All Other Females N=1732	Most Violent Males N=166	All Other Males N=1602
Listen to music	95.8%	96.0%	93.4%	92.9%
Talk to a friend	96.3%	95.2%	84.9%	85.0%
Get angry and yell at people	91.5%	73.9%	85.5%	64.8%
Say something mean to people	90.0%	65.9%	89.2%	65.3%
Use alcohol/drugs	56.8%	27.7%	68.1%	32.1%
Talk to a family member	58.5%	68.5%	57.6%	65.1%
School activities	53.2%	57.1%	46.7%	57.5%
Be with a boyfriend/girlfriend	90.5%	79.2%	88.5%	74.8%
Talk to a teacher, minister, or school counselor	33.7%	34.6%	26.2%	28.9%
Go to church	52.9%	55.9%	47.6%	48.4%
Play sports	60.0%	63.0%	05.5%	86.4%
Sleep	87.9%	86.0%	87.3%	79.4%
Watch T.V.	84.2%	83.1%	82.5%	82.9%
Help others with problems	84.7%	84.6%	59.0%	68.9%
Cry	87.9%	88.2%	32.3%	34.3%
Joke	80.5%	80.7%	86.7%	82.9%
Be by myself	89.5%	90.7%	83.0%	86.4%

endorsed by the aggressive, violent youth compared to their peers, and these can be described as more maladaptive or inappropriate strategies: saying something mean to people, getting angry and yelling, using alcohol or drugs, and being alone with a boyfriend or girlfriend. There are a couple of strategies that are more characteristic of nonviolent youth that can be described as being more positive or adaptive: talking to a family member and participating in a school activity. Some strategies are not different between violent and nonviolent youth but are different for boys and girls: girls are more likely to report going to church, helping others with their problems, and crying. A high percentage of youth reported wanting to be by themselves as a way to cope with stress and violence.

Perhaps one of the most striking things was the strategy that was least endorsed by all youth, regardless of gender and violence: talking to a teacher, minister, or counselor. The theme is pretty clear: aggressive and violent youth are more likely to use maladaptive and inappropriate coping strategies when they are stressed out, increasing the likelihood that their attempts to cope will not work in the short term and may be more harmful in the long term, particularly if they are turning to isolation, drugs, or alcohol as their primary coping strategy. Adolescents who utilize more positive, prosocial coping strategies are better able to build and maintain supportive relationships with others and to be more resilient. These youth have opportunities to develop connections with peers through school activities, with family members (to whom they actually talk), and with positive role models, and they will be able to glean some satisfaction from helping out others in need. All of these strategies will help youth reduce stress and build positive social skills.

In its most basic form, coping with violence reflects how we are able to maintain mental health in the face of everyday exposure to violence, even being victimized by violence on an ongoing basis. No child can do this alone. For those in the most extreme conditions, receiving appropriate, professional treatment and care is essential. For the rest of us, we need to develop and depend upon our social support networks for help. This includes family members, friends, and colleagues. As parents, we can seek to minimize the opportunities our children have for exposure to violence and victimization from violence. Developing appropriate coping strategies can include some of the following general principles to keep in mind:

- Find something that will give you hope and make you feel positively about your life and your future, and then come back to it every day.

- Build your support system, and use it; don't try to do it all on your own. Other people like to be needed and to help when they can; they just need to be asked sometimes.

- Do something nice for someone else or for yourself; create a smile and release some endorphins. It will make your brain feel better.

- Be with someone you care about.

- Keep your sense of humor.

- Fail at something and then tell yourself it's OK.

- Tell your kids that trying their best (effort) is what matters and that having fun while they do something is more important than winning or losing.

- Find a way to take a break. Even five minutes can be refreshing during a stressful day.

- Be humble with your own success and respectful of other's failures. Anyone can enjoy winning, but not everyone can handle losing with dignity.

- Remember that it's all relative. No matter how bad you have it, someone, somewhere, has it worse.

- The person with the most toys at the end doesn't win any game. Even the Joneses (the folks you felt you needed to keep up with) won't care how many toys or how much money you have when you're gone.

- Everybody has something they struggle with, either personally or in their family. I call it hidden psychopathology. There are always skeletons in the closet, so don't be so quick to judge others. Nobody's perfect.

- Sometimes you have to be creative in trying to get your child to talk to you. Be aware, be available, and be patient. Let them come to you in their own way if that is what works for them.

- It's OK to get professional help sometimes. There are some things that moms and dads can't fix for their children, or that their children won't let them fix. Maybe somebody else needs to be the fixer or the one they feel comfortable talking to.

- Learn from the past, but live in the present and look toward the future.

These general principles are helpful reminders to ourselves every once in a while, but what are some specific things parents can do to help their kids deal with the stress of exposure to violence on a daily basis?

- Don't model your own anxiety to your kids. Remaining calm in a difficult situation will be the most important message to show your children how to respond when they are challenged.

- As much as possible, when you are experiencing a crisis, maintain normal daily routines. Children find them comforting in the face of overwhelming stress and unpredictability.

- Turn off the TV. Limit exposure to violent news, shows, movies, videos, and games. Check them out for yourself. National or industry ratings don't always convey enough information about specific content and certainly shouldn't take the place of your values and judgment as a parent.

- Don't make the mistake of thinking a cell phone or pager can take your place as an effective monitor of where your child is or with whom they spend their time.

- Let your children know that you are available to them if they want to talk about something or have questions.

- Notice how your children behave. Watch for signs of stress like nightmares, trouble sleeping, problems with schoolwork or friends, increased irritability, changes in their appetite or eating patterns, depressed mood, stomachaches, becoming overly clingy or anxious about being alone in a room, or asking you lots of questions about "what if this happens." Knowing how they typically behave and react to things will allow you to better recognize when they change and whether the change is a potential problem.

- Reassure your kids that you will keep them safe and secure. Besides you, there are also lots of resources and mechanisms in place to help keep them safe, like police, firefighters, EMS, and the like.

- Have a plan of action in case something happens, just like we prepare our kids in case of a fire in our home. Talk to them about what they can do if they are approached by a stranger, if someone asks them to do something they don't want to do, if someone tries to touch them inappropriately, and so on. Kids feel better if they know what to do rather than feeling scared from not knowing.

- Keep your children informed, but don't go overboard with your actions. You probably don't need to build a bomb shelter and stockpile weapons to prepare for war or disaster; this will likely lead to increased anxiety for kids and establish a climate of persistent fear and paranoia.

- Encourage your children to ask questions about things they hear about on television, see on the Internet, or hear from their friends. I would rather answer their questions as reasonably as I can than leave them guessing or making up their own (maybe inaccurate) answers.

- Always tell your children the truth (but not always with all the messy details) in language and terms they can understand. They're smarter than we give them credit for. They usually know more about what is really going on than we think they do.

- It's OK to say you don't know. No one knows everything. Show your children how to find out accurate information so they can make informed decisions.

Going for a Ride

Sometimes, we all find ourselves in situations that require quick thinking, and we don't always make good decisions. Hindsight of course is twenty-twenty vision, Monday morning quarterbacking, and all those other clichés, but let me tell you a story about what happened to me a few years ago while on a trip to Texas. I made the trip to give talks at a couple of conferences. One talk was on a Monday afternoon, and the other was the first thing Tuesday morning at a separate conference. Since the first conference was over in the late afternoon on Monday, I thought I might be having dinner with some of my hosts. Instead, once my talk was over, one of the hosts turned to me and said, "Well, I have to go teach a class. See you first thing in the morning!" Being flexible in my thinking and wanting to cope appropriately with the situation, I replied, "Sure, no problem. It will be nice to have some down time to relax."

Given all this time I now had on my hands, I sat in the hotel restaurant by myself having dinner. I decided that this would give me an opportunity to make final changes to my remarks for the next morning. Since the hotel was nearby to where I was speaking, a few minutes' walk, I figured I could sleep in the next day (being prepared ahead of time), so I settled in for the night and requested a 7 a.m. wake-up call for the 8 a.m. opening talk I was scheduled to present. I got up right on time, took a leisurely shower, and finished the little bit of packing I had left before I could check out of my room. By this time, it was about 7:25, and I figured I would need to leave by 7:45 to get to the talk with some time to spare. Seeing I had a few more minutes of leisure time left, I thought, "Hey, I'm staying in one of these fancy hotels; I bet they leave a newspaper outside your door in the morning." So, in boxer shorts but nothing else, I stealthily opened the door, seeking to quickly snatch the paper from the floor outside. The paper, however, was not right in front of my door but a couple of feet out into the hallway. No problem. I stuck my foot against my door and bent over to pick up the paper. Of course, when I stood up to reenter my room, I moved my foot, and my hotel door closed firmly into my behind.

OK, so now what do I do? I thought to myself, "Don't panic. You have plenty of time. Just go down by the elevators, call down on the house phone, and ask them to come up and let you back in your room." I gingerly walked down to the end of the hall, hoping no one would come out of a room. I got to the bank of elevators, but alas, there was not a house phone to be found. Now I began getting nervous. Time was running out. There were few choices left. I remembered thinking to myself something like, "Oh well, I'll probably never see any of these people again in my life," as I pushed the button for the elevator. I was going down, literally.

After a few seconds (which seemed more like hours, or at least minutes), the doors to the elevator opened. Of course, there was a young woman on the elevator with her bags, holding a cup of coffee to her lips. There I stood, all of me, with nothing but boxer shorts and the daily paper. The young lady spit out her coffee as I stepped onto the elevator. I brushed past her to the back corner, noticing that there were mirrors on all the walls and ceiling, surrounding me with myself from every angle imaginable. The newspaper was quickly losing its effectiveness as a barrier between my bareness and the rest of the world.

The young lady glanced over at me, a mixture of amusement, pity, and anxiety on her face. Much as I tried to be brave and look straight ahead, I couldn't help but feel her stare. After gliding down a couple of floors, I casually remarked, "Hey, at least you don't have to look at it every day like my wife." This drew a smile and another quick sip of her coffee. Then the doors opened up and a middle-aged man was there waiting to get on the elevator. He, of course, was dressed nicely in an expensive suit with briefcase in tow, quite a contrast to me in my boxers and morning newspaper. He took one step and then stopped, noticing me for the first time. He gave me the full up and down with a quizzical look on his face, to which I firmly and confidently replied, "Yeah, I'm going to start working out." He didn't even smile, but the young lady had now moved from smiling to smirking, and she exchanged that same "I can't believe this guy" look with our new companion on the elevator. Things can't get much worse, I thought to myself.

Well, a few more folks got on the elevator before we hit the lobby, and I have to say that most folks were very polite, holding their tongues and trying not to get too close as the elevator got more crowded. As the elevator doors were mirrored, I could not in good faith reposition my paper, so I let the lookers have their day. OK, so all I have to do now is make my way quickly to the registration desk and get myself another key and get back up to my room and out of the hotel. The doors opened, and much to my chagrin there were about a hundred senior citizens crowding the lobby, waiting to get on a tour bus parked outside. There was nowhere to walk, let alone hide. I began wading my way through the crowd. "Excuse me. Pardon me." The looks turned into gasps as the crowd parted for me to make my way to the front desk. I was now the center of all the attention I was trying to avoid. One older woman yelled out, "What is he doing?" There were whispers and glances and chuckles and raised eyebrows. This was not going well. After what seemed at least four hours (it was more like two minutes), I reached the registration desk. The woman who rode the elevator with me walked up to the clerk a few feet away from me to check out. The young lady (of course) behind the desk looked up to see my glaringly white skin and bright orange boxers (they were a gift). "Can I help you?" she politely asked. "I've locked myself out of my room, and I need a new key," I replied, just as politely. She continued undaunted: "Do you have any form of identification?" This, I thought, would require quite a bit of trickery, but I had none, so I replied in the only way I could: "I have something I can show you, but I don't think you'll want to see it." To this, the woman next to me at the counter turned to the clerk and pleaded, "Just give him a key, will you?" and burst out laughing. No matter, this got me my key, and I darted back to the elevators, feeling many pairs of eyes resting on my backside.

I got myself back up to my room, got dressed, and made my way to the hotel, where the conference organizers were nervously standing on the podium announcing to the crowd, "I'm sure he'll be here. He was here last night," as I walked into the large hall. I told the crowd my story and made my way through my talk before quickly exiting Texas. Suffice it to say that I have not been invited back since that fateful day. It does prove the old adage about Mom telling you to make sure you wear clean underwear.

What does this story have to tell us about coping and problem solving? When I returned home, I had to tell the story to my two boys, who loved the fact that Dad got locked out of his hotel room in nothing but his boxer shorts. They giggled for hours, but that's not the disconcerting part. Upon hearing of my dilemma, Joseph immediately asked, "Dad, why didn't you just knock on someone else's door and ask them to use the phone to call down to the desk?" He was probably seven years old at the time. Patrick, who was five, quickly followed with something like, "Dad, how come you didn't put your pants on before you went out into the hallway to pick up the paper?" They both made good points, and these were things that I had not thought about at all as I found myself in my unforeseen circumstance. Here's the point: sometimes we don't make the best choice in a stressful situation, but we have to make the best of the choices we do make. Even when a situation seems completely out of one's control, it's important to keep things in perspective and maintain one's sense of humor about the predicament. Telling myself (repeatedly in the moment) that (a) I have few options but to act quickly; (b) I'm never going to see these folks again, so it's OK to be embarrassed in front of them; (c) I'm glad I wore clean underwear; and (d) I really have to start working out helped me adapt to what could have been a very stressful and disconcerting event.

CHAPTER TEN

SUGGESTIONS FOR PRACTICE AND POLICY: HOW TO GET HELP WHEN YOU NEED IT

Throughout this book, we've talked about the increasing rates of exposure to violence and its effect on mental health, particularly for young people. We are all exposed to violence on a regular basis, both as witnesses and as victims. Violence has increased in frequency, intensity, immediacy, lethality, and how it impacts our day to-day functioning. In simple terms, violence is everywhere. It is there when we pick up the morning newspaper; it is there when we turn on the television. We can be exposed to violence when we log on to the Internet or when we go to the movies. For our children, violence occurs most often at home, in its most serious form as abuse or neglect, and in its mildest form as chronic arguing, conflict, and fighting between siblings. Violence happens in our neighborhoods and is an increasing problem within the walls of our schools. If violence and exposure to violence is on the rise and its impact on mental health and coping is so significant, how do we get better and improve what's going on? We already covered some specific coping strategies, but what do we do if we need more help with violence or mental health issues? What can we do to reduce exposure to violence and improve mental health? How can we impact practice and policy with respect to violence and mental health? These questions are specifically addressed in this chapter.

First, let's start with some basic information on steps parents or teachers can take if they know of a child who needs help regarding violence or mental health issues. These steps and the information provided here are not meant to replace the need for professional help or intervention. If you

175

think you have a serious problem, seek appropriate assistance as soon as you are able. After we discuss specific action steps to help, we'll end with a section on recommended changes in practice and policy, especially things that we can all advocate for.

What Can I Do If I Think My Child Needs Help?

There are times when we become concerned about how our children are doing, even to the point where we decide that we need some extra help. Here are some basic issues to consider as you develop your plan of action:

1. Make Sure Your Child Is Safe

Above all else, if you think your child is at imminent risk of hurting himself or is being hurt by someone else, seek help and intervention immediately. Take them to the emergency room, call a crisis hotline, or call your local police department or emergency medical service. Safety and security must be your first priority.

2. Call Your Pediatrician or Family Doctor

The family doctor or pediatrician is a good first step to express your concerns. Your visits for other issues like colds, immunizations, or school physicals provide you opportunities to ask questions. The pediatrician should know your child's medical and behavioral history and have a sense of whether your concerns are valid, expectable, within the range of being normal, or a potentially serious problem. Pediatricians see many children every day. While they may not be experts in violence or mental health, they are at least a good barometer of what is happening and an important first step in prevention and identification of potential problems. Medical concerns should always be ruled out first before treating mental health or behavior problems.

3. Contact Your Child's Teacher and School Counselor

Like a pediatrician, schoolteachers see many children of a particular age every day, so they tend to have a pretty good idea of what is normal and expectable behavior. Your child's teacher also spends almost as much time with your child as you do, so he gets to know your child's personality and particular strengths and weaknesses. A teacher can sometimes tell when a child is struggling, doesn't seem to be getting along with others, or is experiencing a change in the quality of his or her schoolwork. These are often red flags for other problems.

4. Contact Your Insurance Provider to Determine Your Coverage and Options

If you find yourself at the point of wanting or needing professional help, make sure you call your insurance company. Plans vary widely in what services they cover, how much they will cover, and the different steps you may need to take to get approval for coverage. Some coverage is limited by the type of presenting problems; other times, limits are based on the number of approved visits or are capped at a certain cost. Some plans require that you go through your pediatrician or another primary-care doctor for a referral. Some plans will only cover services if they are provided by a specialist that belongs to their plan and accepts their payment terms. If you know the limits and boundaries of your plan, you are better able to have an informed discussion with your doctor about treatment planning and options, as well as to be a more effective advocate if you need additional services.

Managed care and the insurance system in general can be extremely complicated and frustrating to deal with. The best thing to do is write down the date and name of whomever you speak to on the phone and record what they tell you to do or what forms they tell you to fill out. Chances are you will be asked for the information at a later time. It is also possible that you will get inaccurate information from someone along the way (because your coverage has changed, you have coverage under a different version of a larger plan, or your provider is no longer part of the network). The main thing to remember is that insurance plans, levels of coverage, requirements to obtain services, and providers all change on a regular basis. You don't want to be without options for help when you need it most.

5. Be Persistent

One message left with a request that a doctor return your phone call may not be enough. You may need to call every day and ask for an appointment. There are many layers to getting help, and you may have to wait what seems like a very long time (several weeks) to get an appointment with an approved provider. Don't give up. It is unlikely that the problem you need help with is going to go away by itself, so even if you have to wait, or if things seem that they are getting better, keep your appointment.

6. Be Patient

It's easy to get frustrated with the system and the long waiting time for help. Remember, it takes many years for a child's behavior to develop, and there are many factors that influence how he may be acting today. It may take more than one visit to a doctor to figure out what is wrong or what to do about it. It will probably take more than a few weeks to change a behavior and ensure that the skills, competencies, and coping strategies are developed enough so that the change will last a long time.

7. Work until You Find the Right Person or Program to Help You and Your Child

Doctors and therapists are a little bit like car mechanics. Most car mechanics specialize in working with certain types or makes of cars or on certain parts of the car. Doctors are the same way. We know that medical doctors specialize on very specific things like surgery, or the heart, or bones. Psychologists, therapists, and counselors are the same way. Most of them specialize by working with a few kinds of problems, by using a very specific approach to therapy, or by confining their work to clients in a specific age group. None are expert at everything. A psychologist who spends most of his time doing marital therapy may not be the right person to help you if your child is five years old and struggling with questions of attention-deficit/hyperactivity disorder. If you meet with a therapist and aren't comfortable with his approach to your problem, if you believe he doesn't have enough experience working with children, or if he doesn't adequately answer your questions or concerns, try to find someone else that you and your child are more comfortable with. If you don't like who is providing your treatment, you will be less likely to go and even less likely to get better.

8. Drugs Don't Cure Everything

Significant advancements have occurred over the last several years in the use of medications to treat a variety of mental health problems for children (e.g., depression, anxiety, obsessive-compulsive thinking), as well as problems related to violence perpetration (e.g., oppositional behavior, aggression, impulse control, hyperactivity, anger management). With appropriate assessment of a problem and a thoughtful approach to treatment planning, medication may be recommended, and it may prove very helpful. However, few mental health or behavior problems are cured completely with the use of medication alone. Almost every study ever done on the issue has shown that a combination of medicines and therapy work better than either one of them alone.

9. Strive for Stability and Predictability

We all do better when we are in circumstances that are more stable and somewhat predictable as opposed to unstable and unpredictable. We feel less anxious when we are secure in our relationships, when we believe that our jobs (and thus our incomes) are stable, and when the world has a sense of calmness. We fear the unknown, and we particularly fear the things that we cannot control. One of the most distressing aspects of the World Trade Center terrorist attacks, besides the obvious impact of such a tragic loss of life, was its unpredictability and the way it violated our basic sense of safety and security. Acts of terrorism may violate our national sense of security, leading to a culture of anxiety and fear, but victimization and exposure to violence on a daily basis can violate our *personal* sense of safety and security. An enormous number of people are victimized by violence every day, and each act of interpersonal violence carries with it the baggage for the victim who has to struggle anew to find a way to cope, to deal with the anger, depression, and anxiety and live with the fear that it could happen again.

When violence affects us culturally or as individuals, we need to try to maintain a sense of predictability and stability for our children. Most of us remember what we were doing the morning of 9-11. I was sitting on the couch watching the morning news. Later that day, I went to pick up our kids from school so that I could talk to them about what they surely had heard about. In fact, the principal at their school had gotten on the loudspeaker during the day asking that the students pray for the victims of this horrible act of violence. While this makes sense to adults who often turn to prayer as a way to cope with and understand violence, my kids were just filled with a sense of anxiety and fear about what had happened, because they knew few of the details of what had happened or why. They just knew that all of the adults around them were very sad and were talking about this unbelievable event.

We spent several minutes sitting in the van, with me trying to explain to them in general terms what had happened. I asked them if they had any questions. I think that part is important. When the unpredictable happens, ask your kids what they want to know. They won't always understand. Be as honest as you can, but there is rarely the need to go into detail about specifics. Your kids do need to know that you're not hiding anything from them (they'll hear about it on the news, from their friends, at school, or in the paper). They need to know that they are safe and that you would never let anything bad happen to them. As much as you can, maintain their daily routine. They'll do better with the consistency and the predictability of their schedule, even if everything around them seems to be in chaos. A basic need for all of us is to feel safe and secure, and if we don't, we need to take action toward that end. No one likes being afraid all the time, feeling out of control, wondering about the unknown.

10. Develop and Use Your Social Network and Support System

Unfortunately, bad things happen. They will happen to all of us, despite our best efforts and intentions. Someone close to us will die. Someone we love will be a victim of violence. We will experience financial hardship, a divorce, or chronic illness. I think we'd make ourselves crazy if we believed we could somehow prevent all of these things from ever happening at some point in our lives. The issue is not one of being able to make these things not happen, because many of them we have no control over. The more relevant challenge is how we handle these events when they do occur. This is one of the hallmarks of coping and maintaining positive mental health over the long term. Being flexible, having high frustration tolerance, maintaining a sense of humor, and keeping things relative—these are the things that help us get through the tough times.

When bad things happen, especially things that make no sense to us, things that we cannot change or control, we feel a deep sense of grief and loss. We feel anxious and depressed. We may feel angry. We may feel a sense of hopelessness about the future. Sometimes things will get better with time—time to understand, time to heal, time to let go of the anger. Other times, things don't get better very quickly, or all of the things we try to make ourselves feel better don't seem to work. This is the time that we need to seek help from others, both formally and informally. This is what happened with our son and his tantrums, which turned out to be related to a problem with reading. The things we tried weren't working. Asking our friends about what to do didn't work. Our son needed more help (or at least different help) than we were able to give him as Mom and Dad. We needed a more formal network of assessment and intervention.

The same concept holds if you or your child begin to feel depressed and don't get better soon. I think we all get depressed once in a while. Often, we have a good reason to feel depressed—we got into a fight with our spouse, the kids are being unruly, our financial situation is stressful, or the dog died. When we can identify a reason for feeling blue, that's a good thing. When we start waking up in the morning feeling depressed all the time and can't really identify why and can't really do anything to make ourselves feel better, then there are questions about whether we need more help in the form of therapy or medicine to help improve or manage our mood. Depression is one of the most commonly occurring mental health issues in this county. Most of us know someone who has taken medicine to relieve symptoms of depression or anxiety. Part of this is probably a reflection of a growing awareness of the problems and better, more effective treatment options, and medicines that relieve symptoms without significant side effects or long-term damage. Part of this is because there is more to be depressed and anxious about. Many of us have not developed very good coping strategies, and we do not take advantage of our support systems, which just leads to increases in our depression and anxiety.

Who makes up our support system? The main players in our informal support system are our family and friends. If you do not get along well with your family and you have a small network of close friends, then your support system when things get rough will be limited. Our extended support system gets more formal and includes our doctors and our child's teachers and the larger systems of care that many of us come in contact with at one point or another: the mental health system, the justice system, the child and family services system, and so on. If we are going to deal with violence and mental health issues, we need to pay ongoing attention to developing and maintaining our informal and formal support systems and use them when we need them. No one can do it all alone. There is no shame in having a child who needs help at some point, whether it is help for academics, mental health, or behavior (or other issues). There is no perfect family, there is no perfect parent, and there is no perfect child.

11. If You Don't Know, Ask Questions and Find Out

If something doesn't seem right with your child's mood or behavior, gather information about what is going on from as many sources and people as you can. Ask your child's teacher how your child is doing in school, academically, socially, emotionally, and behaviorally. If you see an angry, irritable, defiant child at home, does his teacher see the same behavior at school? Has the quality of his academic work changed recently? Does he put forth the same effort that he always did? How is he getting along with other children? When we gather information, we want to know substantively what is going on, but we also want to know if it seems to be happening with lots of different people (adults as well as children, friends as well as strangers) and whether it occurs in many different settings (home as well as school, at a friend's house, in public places in front of strangers, or only with family).

Another reason to gather information is the stress of the unknown. We can't possibly know everything. Remember the family medical dictionary? We now need a family *Physicians' Desk Reference* and a *Diagnostic and Statistical Manual of Mental Disorders*. How are we supposed to know whether our child's irritability is bad enough to need more professional assessment? How are we to know whether our child's skipping over the cracks in the sidewalk is normal or the manifestation of a more serious problem with counting and obsessive behavior? How are we supposed to know whether our child's stomachache and wanting to stay home from school three days in a row is really being sick or is being made up because he wants to avoid the bully who has been taking his lunch money on his walk to school every day? Sometimes we don't know, but today there are many resources, both formal and informal, that we can consult to help us find out. If we try to find out and we still can't figure it out, then it's time to call in a professional.

Having accurate, up-to-date information will help you make informed choices about what the best course of action is for you, your child, and your family. The Internet is an extremely valuable tool for gathering information about a whole host of issues, including things directly related to violence and mental health. If you don't have a computer at your home, most public libraries now have Internet access, as well as many schools. The Internet sites and resources provided as references in the appendix are sites maintained by federal and national professional organizations that have reputations for high standards and high-quality work. Most of the additional resources listed also contain information and links to sources that are not contained elsewhere in this book. Keep in mind, however, that data on the Web changes regularly, and information available on the Internet is difficult to control, so be careful about accepting at face value anything you read or find on the Internet.

12. Make a Coper

As parents, we have lots of opportunities to try to instill in our children the qualities that will help make them effective copers. Certainly personalities come into play here. Some children are temperamentally more easygoing and flexible, while others are much more intense and fixed in the way they do things. However, given their unique personalities, there are many opportunities to help them develop appropriate coping strategies, learn how to use their support system, and become good problem solvers.[1]

You, as a parent, as an adult, can be a powerful socializing tool for children. You can use situations as learning tools to help children become better copers. When a child gets frustrated by a task that is too hard, you can sit with him and talk, just for a few seconds, about what other things he could do to make the task easier. Sometimes it's as simple as taking a break and coming back to it a little later. When your child gets angry and lashes out at a sibling or shoves a piece of furniture, you can talk to him about other ways he can handle his anger more appropriately. Of course, you do this after the time-out and after they've had a chance to cool off. An angry, frustrated child won't hear a thing you're saying. I've sometimes

gone into the three-minute lecture with my children after they have behaved inappropriately, only to hear at the end of my speech, "Are you done
yet, Dad?" They hear none of it. Wait until your child can hear you before
you try to teach them something different.

You can't necessarily make an irritable, aggressive child into a resilient,
easygoing person. You can, however, actively look for those moments and
events that allow you to teach your child ways to better cope with being
angry, frustrated, or upset. You can use moments of grief and confusion to
teach your child that it's OK sometimes to feel sad, but that we can't forget that there are many other things that make us happy. You can reinforce
with your children, often, that they are loved and cared for, and that you
will do everything you can to make sure that they are safe. And, last but
not least, you can tell your children that you will always be there for them
and that they can always talk to you about even the most seemingly unim-
portant thing, not just the really important things. Every once in a while,
they may take you up on it. Be ready to take advantage of every chance
they give you, because there may come a time when they stop asking.

13. Be Hopeful, and Model That Hopefulness to Others

Despite the many challenges we continue to face regarding violence
and mental health, many things have gotten better. We are better at recognizing how violence across settings, both witnessing violence and being
victimized by violence, affects mental health, behavior, and coping. We are
better at recognizing the signs of mental health problems among children
and adolescents. For example, we used to think that toddlers couldn't be
depressed. We know now that depression just looks different developmentally for children than it does for adolescents or adults. We have better treatment options for mental health problems, including many
different options with medicine and better therapies. We know much
more about how brain function and structure are impacted by violence and
how chemicals in the brain contribute to mental health.

The world is a tougher place today, for all of us. I often get asked
when I give a talk whether children and adolescents have it tougher today
than they did twenty or thirty years ago. When I first got asked that question many years ago, I hedged a bit and had to think about it for some
time before answering. Today, my answer is quickly a yes. Things are more

intense today. Access to information and events from around the world is almost immediate. It's harder to protect our kids from the influence of other people, other events, and other opportunities that may get them into trouble. Guns and drugs are much more prevalent today than they were even twenty years ago. Accessibility and opportunity are all around them. The pressure to belong is greater, and the consequences of not fitting in are higher.

Despite all of this, there is much reason to be hopeful about our future. Advances in science and technology are occurring at an unprecedented pace. People live a lot longer than they ever did and have the capacity to stay active and healthy well into their seventh or eighth decade of life. We are much better at understanding what works in preventing violence and at identifying problems with violence and mental health at a much earlier age. The earlier we identify the problems, the quicker we can intervene. The earlier and quicker we intervene, the more likely we are to have success in making things better. Despite the challenges of everyday life, we should be hopeful about what the future holds, and we should model that hopefulness to our children. If they lose hope, what else do they have left but despair? And what kind of world would that be?

What Policies and Practices Need to Change?

There are several practices and policies that we can all engage in or advocate for to make a real difference in the lives of young people. There are more thorough discussions of recommended social policy changes related to violence, mental health, and children available in other publications.[2]

Limit Exposure across Settings

One relatively simple approach to improving child mental health is to limit the ways youth are exposed to violence on an everyday basis. Monitor your child's television viewing and limit the amount of violence young children are exposed to on TV. The average child watches more than two hours of television per day. They are exposed to all sorts of violent behavior, most of it displayed without consequence to the offender. The media often models aggressive behavior as an acceptable way of responding to conflict and as a way to solve problems. Because we often treat movie stars and athletes as role models, children watch them get rewarded for inappropriate behavior. The more violence they watch, the more normal and expectable they view violence, and the more desensitized they get to its effects.

The Internet also preys on young people through unsolicited advertisements, pop-up pornographic sites, unmonitored chat rooms, and an endless network of information, news, gossip, and opportunities for victimization. The violent content and images in movies, PlayStation games, DVDs, and music videos have increased substantially in the past few years. Most industries now rate the content of their products, and this is one source of information about what our children will be exposed to, but ratings are only as good as the person who chooses to enforce the limit. As long as parents buy R-rated violent videos for their eight-year-olds and allow them to regularly watch violent television shows and play violent video games, the industry will continue to make the products and market them to underage audiences.

Early Identification Means a Greater Chance for Success

If there is one common theme of this book, it is that violence is more common, and mental health issues related to exposure to violence more poignant, than most people believe. Under that general theme is emerging research showing that even the earliest exposure to violence (by witnessing chronic violence or being victimized by violence via abuse or neglect) significantly affects brain development, socialization, emotional health, and cognitive skills. Even very young infants and toddlers can be impacted by violence, despite the fact that they cannot talk about their feelings, can't yet draw a picture of what is happening, and may be unable to fully comprehend the nature of what is going on around them. The earlier we notice a young person struggling with mental health and coping or being victimized by violence, the quicker we can intervene to get that child back on the right track. The longer we wait, the more the exposure, risk factors, and challenges accumulate. The longer we wait, the smaller the window of opportunity to effect change, and the task of turning that young person around will be more and more difficult. We can't afford to wait until a child enters elementary school before we become concerned with social development, emotional maturity, and behavior problems. When problems are already present in toddlerhood and the preschool years, they will significantly affect learning, relationships with other adults and peers, and mental health.

Focus on Prevention Because It Works

We can't ignore the person with serious emotional and behavior problems. That person will always need intensive treatment. This could mean medication and therapy or hospitalization. The "deep-end" population of individuals who struggle with violence and serious mental health issues deserves our attention and help. On the other hand, we know that prevention works at reducing later problems with violence and mental health. The earlier we intervene, the better. Prevention efforts that build child competence and social skills are much more effective over time than those that rely on strategies to only reduce risk or seek declines in aggressive or violent behavior. A child who is able to solve problems, who can get along well with others, and who can handle challenges and conflicts without reacting in an impulsive and aggressive manner all the time will do much better over the long term than the child who lacks these skills and is taught only to try to relax when he becomes angry or frustrated. Simple strategies don't always work. For example, counting to ten when an angry, impulsive child gets frustrated will not always keep him from hitting back. People need other coping strategies or other supports available to them when the counting stops and the anger remains.

There are many prevention programs being implemented in schools and other settings that focus on building a child's skills, competencies, character, and coping strategies. More programs are being rigorously tested to show that they result in real, meaningful behavior change. We no longer rely on anecdotal evidence as the gold standard for programs that work. This is a good development for our children and families. Resources are scarce, and we should be implementing only those programs that we have some confidence will work and be effective. Not every program will be effective for every child in every type of school in very different neighborhoods around the country. But we do know much more now about what makes programs work (and kids better) than we did even ten years ago. For example, we're moving more toward models that are universal in nature so that all children are exposed to positive programs early in their development. This is a very different approach than the historical model of doing very little early on and waiting until a behavior or academic or mental health problem gets so bad that a child or family requires extensive (and intensive) intervention or incarceration. By that time, change is much more difficult to accomplish, and the damage is largely done.

Prevention is also about a certain mind-set. As a society, we understand that it takes years to build a road or a highway, and even longer to manufacture a fighter jet. We understand that cities require a strong infrastructure for future growth and stability, and that infrastructure needs to be complemented by a long-term development plan. Why not the same for our children and families? Prevention is hard work and takes a long-term commitment. It's hard to commit to preventing something when the crises and the problems at the deep end keep coming to the fore, requiring our time, our attention, and our resources. Deborah Prothrow-Stith once said that our children will eventually get our time, our attention, and our resources, and it is up to us to decide whether they will get it early, in a preventative and helpful way, or whether they will get it later, when they (and we) are really in trouble, with problems that will be much harder (and more expensive) to fix.

Intervene at Multiple Levels, in Multiple Contexts, and across Multiple Systems

When a child gets to the point of needing additional help with mental health or violence (exposure or behavior), we need to intervene at multiple levels, in multiple contexts, and across multiple systems. Children do not grow up in a vacuum but are directly affected by what goes on in their families, within their peer groups, and in their schools and neighborhoods. Violence and mental health are also impacted by many contextual factors like level of neighborhood disorganization, school climate, the availability of drugs and firearms in a community, the number of adults present on a street to help monitor children, and the level of gang activity. Other structural influences include the role of religion, culture, and acculturation. Finally, no child develops within a single system. Most youth who require intervention are involved in more than one system. This could include schools, the mental health system, the juvenile justice system, public health, or systems that serve children and families. If intervention efforts are going to be successful, they need to address the child's and family's needs across each of these systems, and the systems need to do a better job of coordinating their efforts and sharing information so that we stop duplicating effort. Increasingly limited resources for mental health and substance use treatment require that we do a better job of working together.

Support After-School and Mentoring Programs

Accumulating evidence supports the need to provide after-school services to youth. As noted earlier, the after-school hours are the most dangerous for young people, the time when they are most likely to perpetrate violence, be the victim of violence, or engage in other problem behaviors. Many children are not adequately monitored during these high risk hours of the day. Evidence from the most comprehensive, long-term studies of adolescent health and behavior, like the Add Health project tell us that adult mentors can make a significant difference in the lives of young people. Not all youth have involved, engaged, and caring parents who take an active role in their schoolwork and socialization. For those youth, having any adult who takes an interest in their well-being (including teachers, coaches, relatives, or friends) will significantly improve the chance that they will graduate from high school and grow up to be responsible young adults.

Put Mental Health in the Schools

The evidence is overwhelming: children who stay in school longer and who come from families where academic achievement receives high priority do better across the board as adolescents and young adults than do youth who fail or drop out of school at a young age. Youth who drop out early almost never come back to complete, and once they drop out, they are more likely to be hanging out with other youth who also dropped out. Schools are an excellent place to identify children who need extra help with exposure to violence and mental health issues. One part of the equation is working hard to make schools safe learning environments where youth don't have to worry about being bullied, threatened, or attacked by one of their peers. Creating safe school climates is an essential task of schools today and is the focus of great media attention and federal legislation.

Unfortunately, even within some of the same legislation that focuses on school safety and violence are mandates regarding academic achievement and required testing. Schools currently focus almost all of their available resources on improving academic achievement scores and implementing required testing protocols for their students. Otherwise, an increasingly shrinking tax base and dwindling state-level support for K–12 education has resulted in drastic cutbacks in services, layoffs of staff, and elimination of most core programs related to reduction of violence or mental health services. Unless a service can be directly tied to academic success and achievement, it receives little priority in today's schools. Of course, child mental health is critical to ensuring academic success, but the link is not as obvious as, say, the link between truancy and academic achievement; if a child is not attending school, how can he get good grades? The same is not true regarding mental health and academic success; an anxious or depressed child may not be working to his full potential but still may be an average student or able to perform enough to get by.

More schools today recognize the value of placing social workers or other mental health professionals directly in the school as a resource for identifying students with mental health needs, assessing risk, and providing referrals to community-based agencies for additional treatment. This is different from having school-based mental health professionals provide therapy at school. Few schools would have the resources to fund several full-time professionals to provide high-level individual or group therapy. The traditional guidance counselor is also generally ill equipped to handle the serious mental health and behavior issues many students present with today. Short of having a psychiatrist on staff, few nurses are able to do much more than monitor the psychiatric medications many students take during the school day.

The primary role of a school is academic achievement, and we should not lose sight of that. Schools cannot be surrogate families or replace the important role of parents in a child's socialization and development, but the reality is that students bring their own histories, personalities, mental health issues, behaviors, and risk and protective factors into the classroom with them. Schools (particularly teachers) need to find ways to help children interact with their peers in the classroom successfully so that all children have an opportunity to learn and to succeed. It only takes one highly disruptive child to affect learning in an entire classroom. The reality is that schools have been forced to take on more roles than the traditional responsibilities for which they exist. Schools are microcosms of the communities and populations they serve. Neighborhood problems don't evaporate once students walk through the doors of a building. Sometimes those problems (ethnic or cultural clashes, for example) are exacerbated when students are in a confined place together. The conundrum of choosing between prevention versus more intensive services arises in part because schools are forced to prioritize their use of limited resources to handle those that are most problematic in their building. Sometimes this is bullying, and sometimes it is vandalism. Sometimes it is creating a culture of safety and security, and sometimes it is substance use or violence. All of these factors influence learning and impact child mental health.

We Need a National Effort to Improve and Support Parenting

Parents, and parenting, matter. There is no more direct way to say it. Parents or other adult primary caregivers are the most important factor in a child's development and socialization. All of the research on child mental health and violence back this up. You've heard the analogies before. We require youth to pass a test to get a driver's license. We require tests for graduating from school. We require the demonstration of competency before a person is allowed to purchase a firearm. Professionals are required to obtain continuing education in order to maintain their license. This is true of schoolteachers, accountants, psychologists, medical doctors, engineers, Realtors, and many other professionals. Why is it, then, that our most important profession, parenting, requires nothing but the biological means to conceive a child? Most of us learn about being parents from our own parents, but what do we do if our own parents weren't very good at it, if our parents got divorced, or if we grew up with only one parent as a model?

I think it is time to consider a national effort that focuses on improved parenting skills. This would be more than making parenting classes or child development courses a requirement in high schools, although that would be a good start. I'm sure there would be considerable debate about that and about whether someone (a government or some other entity) has the right to dictate the type of curriculum that is taught in a public or private school. Consider the debate that has occurred over many years regarding the role of religion in school curricula, and more recently the debate in several states about the inclusion of creationism versus evolutionary theory in science class. So, I'm not sure that mandating a parenting class to all teens in high school would work. Some would argue that the teens most at risk for early pregnancy and parenthood are the ones who dropped out of school long before high school anyway.

Another alternative is to require individuals to take a class on effective parenting after they know they are pregnant, at least for their first child (although a refresher for subsequent children wouldn't hurt). Most hospitals, for example, require participating in birthing classes if a couple is planning to deliver a baby at their facility. Many religious denominations encourage couples to undergo some formal discussion of their commitment to marriage and their interest in starting a family. You could easily integrate parenting courses into hospital procedures as one of the options presented to parents after the birth of their child, or you could encourage faith-based organizations to integrate parenting into their work with couples planning to marry.

A more formal system of parenting support could be sponsored by government agencies in much the same way that health departments or county systems pay for programs like home visits by nurses to mothers of high-risk infants. In one type of program, nurses will come to your home on a regular basis for two to three years to check on the baby's growth and development and to provide some unstructured support around parenting and child-care issues. This type of program has been extensively tested in several studies and has been shown to reap significant benefits years later with respect to increased academic achievement, reductions in a family's use of public support systems, and reduced risk of a child ending up delinquent.

A similar kind of program could be instituted for all new parents on the birth of their first child: regular visits to the home by a child development/ parenting expert who provides assistance, support, and information regarding child development and parenting. This program could be expanded so that a family receives twice-annual home visits to discuss parenting and developmental issues all the way through high school. If every state adopted such a program, services could be systematized across communities so that even if a family moves to another city or state, they could receive the same kinds of ongoing support and assistance. One would receive the help automatically until all children made it through high school.

Of course, these programs are politically and practically ambitious. It would take enormous social shift and political will to accomplish such a wide-ranging and expensive initiative. Resources would have to be dramatically redirected. For example, over the last twenty years, state funding for prisons has replaced funding for education and health as the number one expense in most states. We like to feel safe, and it is politically expedient to put most offenders, violent or not, behind bars for many years. Few would argue about the need to incarcerate violent offenders, but there are new initiatives to divert nonviolent drug offenders from prison into treatment via specialized drug courts, and even offenders with serious mental health problems to treatment via specialized mental health courts. Most of these programs are driven by cost rather than compassion or some political agenda. The cost of incarcerating one individual for one year is about $30,000 in most states. This is far more than even the most intensive, ambitious, comprehensive treatment plan. If the recidivism rates (the chances a person will reoffend) for incarceration versus treatment are even close, why not choose treatment? The chance that an offender will improve with treatment are much greater than hoping they will improve after being incarcerated in prison for several years. The fact remains that most offenders eventually get released from prison, as few are sentenced for the rest of their lives. When they get out, they almost invariably return to their old neighborhoods. Without proper support, education, training, and treatment, their risk of reoffending remains high. There is increased emphasis today on offender reentry programs, trying to ease the transition of offenders from prison back into a productive adult life.

The bottom line is that we could support universal parenting programs for all new parents if we really wanted to. The question remains, however, whether we believe it important enough to expend the time, energy, and resources to make it happen. Think of how much better children and families would fare if such a thing were to happen everywhere. Parents could learn about how to effectively monitor their children, and they could learn about appropriate discipline styles and strategies. They could hear about how what they do and say in front of their children can affect their child's brain chemistry and circuitry, and about how their child learns to solve problems and deal with frustration. They could learn how to effectively communicate with their children, how to use teachable moments, and how be involved (vs. just being available) with their children. Parents could learn about what to expect in normal development so they can take action if something appears to be going awry, and they could learn about how relationships change over time as their child gets older and more mature. Parents could learn how effort is just as important as outcome and how their own genetic makeup may influence their child's personality, behavior, ability to achieve, and long-term development. Parents could learn how to be good parents. How neat would that be?

Mental Health Is Just as Important as Physical Health

Most of our health care plans cover services and treatment for physical illness and injury. Recent government commissions have called for significant changes in health care policy to make mental health treatment benefits similar to the benefits we receive for physical health.[3] On a conceptual level, few would disagree that mental health is just as important as physical health. From a societal perspective, however, physical illness or injury usually has a defined, fixed treatment. For most illnesses, the patient gets better, or there is a medicine that offers a cure. Mental health isn't like that. It's much more unpredictable, variable, and difficult to treat in a specific amount of time or with a set dose of a medicine. The perception is that most insurers don't want to provide comprehensive mental health benefits because the cost and management of treatment options would be a tremendous burden and very difficult to predict. This would wreak havoc on most insurance-company profit projections. One of the biggest problems with managed care and mental health treatment is the industry's attempt to manage (i.e., limit) treatment options for mental health care. In most circumstances, a clinician has to complete a tremendous amount of paperwork documenting the need for treatment or further assessment, justifying each treatment choice and course. This is much different than a physician writing down a code number for a physical ailment that has a prescribed, well-accepted course of treatment (they still don't pay for "experimental" treatments for most physical illnesses). The problem is that most mental health problems are not fixable over a set number of therapy sessions or over a specific (usually short) period of time. Who decided that depression should be cured in ten sessions or that marital conflict could be eased and a relationship saved in six visits? The current model emphasizes quick treatment, a dependence on medicines over therapy, and a focus on crisis management. Long-term functioning and coping as treatment goals are not usually on the radar screen.

What Does the Future Hold?

Despite the many challenges we face in addressing the complex problem of violent behavior and its affect on mental health, there exist many new and exciting advances in our understanding of the factors that influence child health and well-being. Research on brain growth and development, for example, holds much promise in helping us better understand the impact of violence exposure and victimization, as well as mental health problems like depression and anxiety. A better understanding of the functions and chemical makeup of the brain has helped us develop more effective medications to improve mental health symptoms, for example. Improved technology like computerized imaging and brain mapping has also significantly influenced advances in treatment. We also know more today than ever before about how genes influence personality, behavior, and mental health. Genetic testing and research with stem cells holds real promise for treating life-threatening and life-altering disorders, and eventually these same strategies may be helpful in treating the chemical or genetic factors that influence violent behavior and mental health.

Slowly but surely, we are recognizing the need to take a long-term view with a focus on prevention. Focusing on prevention, a more proactive stance, rather than on reactionary measures like suppression and incarceration, is not a quick fix, and it is not an approach that tends to lead to immediate, observable change. This is where we need to be patient, persistent, and committed. Prevention is more effective and more cost efficient than a back-end (or deep-end) approach that waits until a youth is so deeply involved with violence or serious mental health problems that he is almost surely a candidate for long-term treatment, residential care, or incarceration. Prevention is not a luxury but a necessity for us to help make sure that whatever we change is sustained for the long term. Our children deserve our commitment to the long term. Their future depends on it.

APPENDIX

Additional Resources Not Referenced in the Text

Bosworth, K. (2000). Protective schools: Linking drug abuse prevention with student success. University of Arizona, The Arizona Board of Regents. Available at www.drugstats.org.

Dwyer, K., Osher, D., & Warger, C. (1998). *Early warning, timely response: A guide to safe schools.* Washington, DC: U.S. Department of Education. Available at http://cecp.air.org/guide.

Dwyer, K., & Osher, D. (2000). *Safeguarding our children: An action guide.* Washington, DC: U.S. Departments of Education and Justice, American Institutes for Research.

Flannery, D. (1997). *School violence: Risk, preventive intervention and policy.* Monograph for the Institute of Urban and Minority Education, Columbia University and the ERIC Clearinghouse for Education, Urban Diversity Series No. 109.

Flannery, D., & Huff, C. R. (Eds.). (1999). *Youth violence: Prevention, intervention and social policy.* Washington, DC: American Psychiatric Press.

Flannery, R. B. (1999). *Preventing youth violence: A guide for parents, teachers, and counselors.* New York: Continuum.

Gullotta, T. P., & McElhaney, S. J. (Eds.). (1999). *Violence in homes and communities: Prevention, intervention and treatment.* With the National Mental Health Association. Thousand Oaks, CA: Sage.

Institute for American Values. (2003). *Hardwired to connect: The new scientific case for authoritative communities.* With Dartmouth Medical School and YMCA of the USA. Author.

Jensen, E. (1998). *Teaching with the brain in mind.* Alexandria, VA: Association for Supervision and Curriculum Development. Kellam, S., Prinz, R., & Sheley, J. (2000). *Preventing school violence: Plenary papers of the 1999 conference on criminal justice research and evaluation—enhancing policy and practice through research,* vol. 2. Washington, DC: U.S. Department of Justice, Office of Justice Programs, National Institute of Justice.

Muckenhoupt, M. (2002). *Mental health issues in schools: A guide for teachers, school administrators, and parents.* Education Development Center.

National Center for Injury Prevention and Control. (2000). *Best practices of youth violence prevention: A source book for community action.* Atlanta, GA: Centers for Disease Control and Prevention.

National Clearinghouse on Families & Youth. (1996). Supporting your adolescent: Tips for parents. Washington, DC: U.S. Department of Health and Human Services; Administration for Children and Families; Administration on Children, Youth and Families; Family and Youth Services. Available at www.ncfy.com.

National Crime Prevention Council. (2003). *School safety and security tool kit: A guide for parents, schools, and communities.* Washington, DC: NCPC.

National Institute on Drug Abuse. (2002). Mind over matter: The brain's response to drugs—teacher's guide (revised). Washington, DC: U.S. Department of Health and Human Services; National Institutes of Health; National Institute on Drug Abuse.

Osofsky, J. (Ed.). (1997). *Children in a violent society.* New York: Guilford.

Public Agenda. (2002). *A lot easier said than done: Parents talk about raising children in today's America.* New York: Author.

Resnick, M. D., Bearman, P. S., Blum, R. W., Bauman, K. E., Harris, K. M., Jones, J., et al. (1998). Protecting adolescents from harm: Findings from the National Longitudinal Study on Adolescent Health. *Journal of the American Medical Association, 278,* 823–832. *Safe and sound: An educational leader's guide to evidence-based social and emotional learning (SEL) programs.* March 2003.

SAMHSA. (2000). *The CMHS approach to enhancing youth resilience and preventing youth violence in schools and communities.* Washington, DC: Author. Available at www.mentalhealth.org.

Singer, M., & Flannery, D. (Eds.). (2004). Community violence [special issue]. *Journal of Community Psychology, 32,* 489–641.

Trickett, P., & Schellenbach, C. (Eds.). (1998). *Violence against children in the family and the community.* Washington, DC: American Psychological Association.

U.S. Department of Health and Human Services. (1999). *Mental health: A report of the surgeon general.* Rockville, MD: U.S. Department of Health and Human Services, Substance Abuse and Mental Health Services Administration, Center for Mental Health Services, National Institutes of Health, National Institute of Mental Health.

U.S. Department of Health and Human Services. (2001). *Youth violence: A report of the surgeon general.* Rockville, MD: U.S. Department of Health and Human Services, Centers for Disease Control and Prevention, National Center for Injury Prevention and Control; Substance Abuse and Mental Health Services Administration, Center for Mental Health Services.

Weissberg, R., & Kumpfer, K. (Eds.). (2003). Prevention that works for children and youth: Special issue. *American Psychologist, 58,* 425–490.

Websites for Federal Agencies and National Organizations

American Academy of Child and Adolescent Psychiatry
www.aacap.org

American Academy of Pediatrics
www.aap.org

American Psychiatric Association
www.psych.org

American Psychological Association
www.apa.org

American School Counselor Association
www.schoolcounselor.org

Centers for Disease Control and Prevention, Division of Violence Prevention
www.cdc.gov/ncipc/dvp/dvp.htm

Center for Mental Health Services
www.mentalhealth.org/cmhs

ERIC Clearinghouse
www.aspensys.com/eric
The ERIC database includes research reports, publications, studies, and journal access for school safety and security, school violence, legal issues, and mental health.

APPENDIX

Federation of Families for Children's Mental Health
www.ffcmh.org/enghome.htm

National Alliance for the Mentally Ill (NAMI)
www.nami.org.

National Association of School Psychologists
www.naspweb.org

National Crime Prevention Council
www.ncpc.org

National Education Association
www.nea.org

National Institutes of Mental Health
www.nimh.nih.gov

National Mental Health Association
www.nmha.org

National PTA
www.pta.org.index.stm

Office of Juvenile Justice and Delinquency Prevention
http://ojjdp.ncjrs.org

Office of Safe and Drug Free Schools
U.S. Department of Education
www.ed.gov/offices/OESE/SDFS

Partnerships Against Violence Network (PAVNET)
www.pavnet.org

Prevention First
www.prevention.org

School Social Work Association of America
www.sswaa.org

U.S. Department of Education
www.ed.gov

U.S. Department of Justice
www.usdoj.gov

U.S. Department of Health and Human Services
www.hhs.gov

NOTES

Chapter 1

1. Finkelhor, D., & Dziuba-Leatherman, J. (1994). Victimization of children. *American Psychologist* 49:173–83.

2. Singer, M., & Flannery, D. (2000). The relationship between children's threats of violence and violent behavior. *Archives of Pediatrics and Adolescent Medicine* 154:785–90.

Chapter 2

1. Gale, C. R., O'Callaghan, F., Godfrey, K., Law, C., & Martyn, C. (2004). Critical periods of brain growth and cognitive function in children. *Brain* 127:321–29.

2. Perry, B. (2002). Childhood experience and the expression of genetic potential: What childhood neglect tells us about nature and nurture. *Brain and Mind* 3:1.

3. Kotulak, R. (1997). *Inside the brain: Revolutionary discoveries of how the mind works.* Kansas City, MO: Andrews McNeel.

4. Perry, B. (2002). Childhood experience and the expression of genetic potential: What childhood neglect tells us about nature and nurture. *Brain and Mind* 3:1.

5. Bruer, J. (2001). *A critical and sensitive period primer: Critical thinking about critical periods.* Boston, MA: Paul H. Brooks.

6. Perry, B. (1997). Incubated in terror: Neurodevelopmental factors in the 'cycle of violence.' In J. Osofsky (Ed.), *Children in a violent society* (pp. 124–49). New York: Guilford.

7. Chugani, D. C., et al. (2001); Rutter, English, et al. (1998); Chugani, H. T., Behen, M. E., Muzik, O., Juhasz, C., Nagy, F., & Chugani, D. C. (2001). Local brain functional activity following early deprivation: A study of post-institutionalized Romanian orphans. *Neuroimage* 14:1290–1301; Rutter, M., & English and Romanian Adoptees Study Team. (1998). Developmental catch-up, and deficit, following adoption after severe global early deprivation. *Journal of Child Psychology and Psychiatry* 39:465–76.

8. Dawson, G., Frey, K., Pangiotides, H., Osterling, J., & Hessl, D. (1997). Infants of depressed mothers exhibit atypical frontal brain activity: A replication and extension of previous findings. *Journal of Child Psychology and Psychiatry and Allied Disciplines* 38:179–86.

9. Durston, S. (2001). Anatomical MRI of the developing human brain: What have we learned? *Journal of the American Academy of Child and Adolescent Psychiatry* 40:1012–20.

10. Geidd, J., et al. (1999). Brain development during childhood and adolescence: A longitudinal MRI study. *Nature Neuroscience* 2:861–63.

11. Yurgelun-Todd, D. (2002). Sex differences in cerebral tissue volume and cognitive performance during adolescence. *Psychological Reports* 91:743–57.

12. Chambers, R., Taylor, J., & Potenza. (2003). Developmental neurocircuitry of motivation in adolescence: A critical period of addiction vulnerability. *American Journal of Psychiatry* 160:1041–52.

13. Chung, M., et al. (2003). Deformation-based surface morphometry applied to gray matter deformation. *Neuroimage* 18:198–213.

14. Harris, J. (1998). *The nurture assumption: Why children turn out the way they do.* New York: Free Press.

15. Rowe, D. (1997). *The Limits of Family Influence.* New York: Guilford.

16. Caspi, A., Sugden, K., Moffitt, T., et al. (2003). Influence of life stress on depression: Moderation by a polymorphism in the 5-HTT gene. *Science* 301:386–89.

17. *Science,* July 19, 2002, p. 400; Holden, C. (2003). Getting the short end of the allele. *Science,* July 18: 291–93.

18. Chambers, R., Taylor, J., & Potenza. (2003). Developmental neurocircuitry of motivation in adolescence: A critical period of addiction vulnerability. *American Journal of Psychiatry* 160:1041–52.

19. Perry, B. (2002). Childhood experience and the expression of genetic potential: What childhood neglect tells us about nature and nurture. *Brain and Mind* 3:1.

20. Hay, D. F., Pawlby, S., Angold, A., Harold, G., & Sharp, D. (2003). Pathways to violence in children of mothers who were depressed postpartum. *Developmental Psychology* 39:1083–94.

21. See note 17.

22. Cowley, G. (2003, February). Our bodies, our fears. *Newsweek*, 43–49.

23. Perry, B. (2002). Childhood experience and the expression of genetic potential: What childhood neglect tells us about nature and nurture. *Brain and Mind* 3:1.

Chapter 3

1. Flannery, D. (1997). *School violence: Risk, preventive intervention and policy.* ERIC Clearinghouse on Urban Education, Urban Diversity Series No. 109. Institute for Urban and Minority Education, Columbia University.

2. Hack, M., Flannery, D., Schluchter, M., Cartar, L., Borawski, E., & Klein, N. (2002). Young adult outcomes of very low birth weight children. *New England Journal of Medicine* 346:149–57.

3. Loeber, R., & Stouthamer-Loeber, M. (1998). Development of juvenile aggression and violence: Some misconceptions and controversies. *American Psychologist* 53:242–459.

4. Patterson, G., DeBaryshe, D., & Ramsey, B. (1989). A developmental perspective on antisocial behavior. *American Psychologist* 44:329–35.

5. Moffitt, T. (1993). Adolescence-limited and life-course-persistent antisocial behavior: A developmental taxonomy. *Psychology Review* 100:674–701; Moffitt, T., Caspi, A., Dickson, N., Silva, P., & Stanton, W. (1996). Childhood-onset versus adolescent-onset antisocial conduct problems in males: Natural history from ages 3 to 18 years. *Development and Psychopathology* 8:399–424.

6. American Psychological Association. (1993). *Summary report of the American Psychological Association Commission on violence and youth.* Washington, DC: American Psychological Association.

7. Singer, M., Miller, D., Guo, S., Flannery, D., Frierson, T., & Slovak, K. (1999). Contributors to violent behavior among elementary and middle school children. *Pediatrics* 104:878–84.

8. Meltzer, L. J., Levine, M. D., Karniski, W., Palfreg, J. S., & Clarke, S. (1984). An analysis of the learning style of adolescent delinquents. *Journal of Learning Disabilities* 17:600–18.

9. Zagar, R., Arbit, J., Hughes, J. R., Busell, R. E., & Busch, K. (1989). Developmental and disruptive behavior disorders among delinquents. *Journal of the American Academy of Child and Adolescent Psychiatry* 28:437–40.

10. Bryant, A. L., Schulenberg, J., Bachman, J. G., O'Malley, P. M., & Johnston, L. D. (2000). Understanding the links among school misbehavior, academic achievement, and cigarette use: A national panel study of adolescents. *Prevention Science* 1:71–87.

11. U.S. Department of Education. (2002). *Indicators of school crime and safety: 2002.* Washington, DC: U.S. Department of Justice, Office of Justice Programs.

12. McEvoy, A., & Welker, R. (2000). Antisocial behavior, academic failure, and school climate: A critical review. *Journal of Emotional and Behavioral Disorders* 8:130–40.

Chapter 4

1. Patterson, G., DeBaryshe, B., & Ramsey, E. (1989). A developmental perspective on antisocial behavior. *American Psychologist* 44:329–35; Patterson, G. (1982). *A social learning approach to family intervention: III. Coercive family process.* Eugene, OR: Castalia.

2. Baumrind, D. (1989). Rearing competent children. In W. Damon (Ed.), *Child development today and tomorrow* (pp. 349–78). San Francisco: Jossey-Bass; Lamborn, S. D., Mounts, N. S., Steinberg, L., & Dornbusch, S. M. (1991). Patterns of competence and adjustment among adolescents from authoritative, authoritarian, indulgent, and neglectful families. *Child Development* 62:1049–65.

3. Flannery, D., Williams, L., & Vazsonyi, A., (1999). Who are they with and what are they doing? Delinquent behavior, substance use and early adolescents' after-school time. *American Journal of Orthopsychiatry* 69:247–53.

Chapter 5

1. Singer, M., Anglin, T., Song, L., & Lunghofer, L. (1995). Adolescents' exposure to violence and associated symptoms of psychological trauma. *Journal of the American Medical Association* 273:477–82; Flannery, D., Singer, M., & Wester, K. (2003). Violence, coping and mental health in a community sample of adolescents. *Violence and victims* 10:403–18.

2. Singer, M., Miller, D., Guo, S., Flannery, D., Frierson, T., & Slovak, K. (1999). Contributors to violent behavior among elementary and middle school children. *Pediatrics* 104:878–84.

3. Osofsky, J., Wewers, S., Hann, D., & Frick, A. (1993). Chronic community violence: What is happening to our children? *Psychiatry* 56:36–45.

4. Taylor, L., Zuckerman, B., Harik, V., & Groves, B. (1994). Witnessing violence by young children and their mothers. *Developmental and Behavioral Pediatrics* 15:120–23.

5. Drotar, D., Flannery, D., et al. (2003). Identifying and responding to the mental health service needs of children who have experienced violence: A community-based approach. *Clinical Child Psychology and Psychiatry* 9:187–204.

6. Osofsky, J. (1995). The effects of exposure to violence on young children. *American Psychologist* 50:782–88; Pynoos, R. S. (1993). Traumatic stress and developmental psychopathology in children and adolescents. In J. M. Oldham, M. B. Riba & A. Tasman (Eds.), *American Psychiatric Press Review of Psychiatry* (vol. 12). Washington, DC: American Psychiatric Press; Finkelhor, D. (1995). The victimization of children: A developmental perspective. *American Journal of Orthopsychiatry* 65:177–93.

7. Drotar, Flannery, et al. (2003) Identifying and responding to the mental health service needs of children who have experienced violence: A community-based approach. *Clinical Child Psychology and Psychiatry* 9:187–204.

8. Institute for the Study and Prevention of Violence. (2002). *Children who witness violence program year 2 final report (December, 2002).* Kent State University: Author.

9. Liebert, R., & Sprafkin, J. (1988). *The early window: Effects of television on children and youth,* (3rd ed.). Elmsford, NY: Pergamon.

10. Huston, A., Donnerstein, E., Fairchild, H., et al. (1992). *Big world, small screen: The role of television in American society.* Lincoln, NE: University of Nebraska Press.

11. Comstock, G. A., & Paik, H. (1991). *Television and the American child.* San Diego, CA: Academic Press.

12. Huesmann, R., Moise-Titus, J., Podolski, C., & Eron, L. (2003). Longitudinal relations between children's exposure to TV violence and their aggressive and violent behavior in young adulthood: 1977–1992. *Developmental Psychology* 39:201–21.

13. Johnson, J., Cohen, P., Smailes, E., Kasen, S., & Brook, J. (2002). Television viewing and aggressive behavior during adolescence and adulthood. *Science* 295:2468–71.

14. Christakis, D., Zimmerman, G., DiGuiseppe, D., & McCarty, C. (2004). Early television exposure and subsequent attentional problems in children. *Pediatrics* 113:708–13.

Chapter 6

1. Shannon, D. (1998). *No, David.* New York: Scholastic.

2. Chambers, R., Taylor, J., & Potenza. (2003). Developmental neurocircuitry of motivation in adolescence: A critical period of addiction vulnerability. *American Journal of Psychiatry* 160:1041–52.

3. Flannery, D., Montemayor, R., Eberly, M., & Torquati, J. (1993). Unraveling the ties that bind: Affective expression and perceived conflict in parent-adolescent interactions. *Journal of Social and Personal Relationships* 10:495–509.

4. Foshee, V., Bauman, K., Arriaga, X., Helms, R., Koch, G., & Linder, G. F. (1998). An evaluation of Safe Dates, an adolescent dating violence prevention program. *American Journal of Public Health* 88:45–50; Silverman, J., et al. (2001). Dating violence against adolescent girls and associated substance use, unhealthy weight control, sexual risk behavior, pregnancy, and suicidality. *Journal of the American Medical Association* 286:572–79.

5. Flannery, D., Huff, C. R., & Manos, M. (1994). Youth gangs: A developmental perspective. In Gullotta, T., Adams, G., & Montemayor, R. (Eds.), *Delinquent, violent youth: Theory and interventions* (pp. 175–204). Thousand Oaks, CA: Sage.

6. Wilkinson, D., & Fagan, J. (2001). What we know about gun use among adolescents. *Clinical Child and Family Psychology Review* 4:109–32.

7. Miller, M., Azrael, D., & Hemenway, D. (2002). Firearm availability and unintentional firearm deaths, suicide, and homicide among 5–14 year olds. *The Journal of Trauma, Injury, Infection and Critical Care* 52:267–75.

8. Hennes, H. (1998). A review of violence statistics among children and adolescents in the United States. In Hennes & Calhoun (Eds.), Violence among children and adolescents, *The Pediatric Clinics of North America* 45(2), 269–80.

9. Center for Disease Control and Prevention. (1997). Rates of homicide, suicide, and firearm-related deaths among children, 26 industrialized countries. *MMWR* 46:101–5.

10. Center for Disease Control and Prevention. (1997). Rates of homicide, suicide, and firearm-related deaths among children, 26 industrialized countries. *MMWR* 46:101–5.

11. Escobado, L. G., Reddy, M., & DuRant, R. H. (1997). Relationship between cigarette smoking and health risk and problem behaviors among US adolescents. *Archives of Pediatrics and Adolescent Medicine* 151:66–77.

12. Flannery, D., Vazsonyi, A., Torquati, J., & Fridrich, A. (1994). Ethnic and gender differences in risk for early adolescent substance use. *Journal of Youth and Adolescence* 23:195–213.

Chapter 7

1. U.S. Department of Education. (2002). *Indicators of school crime and safety: 2002.* Washington, DC: U.S. Department of Justice, Office of Justice Programs.

2. Kachur, S., Stennies, G., Kenneth, E., Modzeleski, W., Stephenson, R., Murphy, R., Kresnow, M., Sleet, D., & Lowry, R. (1996). School associated violent deaths in the United States, 1992 to 1994. *Journal of the American Medical Association* 275:1729–33.

3. Anderson, M., Kaufman, J., Simon, T., Barrios, L., Paulozzi, L., Ryan, G., Hammond, R., Modzeleski, W., Feucht, T., Potter, L., & the School-Associated

Violent Deaths Study Group. (2001). School-associated violent deaths in the United States, 1994–1999. *Journal of the American Medical Association* 286:2695–2702.

4. Centers for Disease Control and Prevention. (2001). Temporal variations in school-associated student homicide and suicide events—United States, 1992–1999. *MMWR* 50(31), 657–60.

5. Nansel, T., Overpeck, M., Pilla, R., Ruan, W., Simons-Morton, B., & Scheidt, P. (2001). Bullying behaviors among US youth: Prevalence and association with psychosocial adjustment. *Journal of the American Medical Association* 285:2094–2100.

6. Olweus, D. (1993). *Bullying at school: What we know and what we can do.* Oxford, England: Blackwell.

7. Singer, M., & Flannery, D. (2000). The relationship between children's threats of violence and violent behavior. *Archives of Pediatrics and Adolescent Medicine* 154:785–90; Liau, A., Flannery, D., & Quinn-Leering, K. (2004). A comparison of teacher-rated and self-reported threats of interpersonal violence. *Journal of Early Adolescence* 24:231–49.

8. Singer, M., Miller, D., Guo, S., Flannery, D., Frierson, T., & Slovak, K. (1999). Contributors to violent behavior among elementary and middle school children. *Pediatrics* 104:878–84; Flannery, D., Wester, K., & Singer, M. (2004). Impact of exposure to violence in school on child and adolescent mental health and behavior. *Journal of Community Psychology* 32:559–74.

9. Thornberry, T. P. (1994). *Violent families and youth violence.* Washington, DC: Department of Justice, Office of Justice Programs, National Institute of Justice.

10. Moses, A. (1999). Exposure to violence, depression, and hostility in a sample of inner city high school youth. *Journal of Adolescence* 22:21–32.

11. Flannery, D., Singer, M., & Wester, K. (2001). Violence exposure, psychological trauma, and suicide risk in a community sample of dangerously violent adolescents. *Journal of the American Academy of Child and Adolescent Psychiatry* 40:435–42.

12. McEvoy, A., & Welker, R. (2000). Antisocial behavior, academic failure, and school climate: A critical review. *Journal of Emotional and Behavioral Disorders* 8:130–40.

Chapter 8

1. Garbarino, J. (1999). *Lost boys: Why our sons turn violent and how we can save them.* New York: Free Press.

2. Flannery, D., Singer, M., & Wester, K. (2001). Violence exposure, psychological trauma, and suicide risk in a community sample of dangerously violent adolescents. *Journal of the American Academy of Child and Adolescent Psychiatry* 40:435–42.

3. *New York Times*, April 9, 2000.

4. Davies, M., and Flannery, D. (1998). Post-traumatic stress disorder in children and adolescents exposed to violence. In H. Hennes & A. Calhoun (Eds.), Violence among children and adolescents, *Pediatric Clinics of North America* 45:341–53.

5. National Center for Health Statistics. (2002). *Health, United States, 2002.* Washington, DC: U.S. Department of Health and Human Services.

6. New Zealand Health Information Service. (2001). *New Zealand Ministry of Health: Suicide Trends in New Zealand 1978–1998.* Wellington, New Zealand: Author.

7. Beautrais, A. (2003). Suicide and serious suicide attempts in youth: A multiple-group comparison study. *American Journal of Psychiatry* 160:1093–99.

8. Virkkuen et al. (1995). Low brain serotonin turnover rate (low CSF 5-HIAA) and impulsive violence. *Journal of Psychiatry and Neuroscience* 20:271–75.

Chapter 9

1. Singer, M., Anglin, T., Song, L., & Lunghofer, L. (1995). Adolescents' exposure to violence and associated symptoms of psychological trauma. *Journal of the American Medical Association* 273:477–482; Flannery, D., Singer, M., & Wester, K. (2003). Violence, coping and mental health in a community sample of adolescents. *Violence and victims* 10:403–18.

Chapter 10

1. Rutter, M. (1987). Psychosocial resilience and protective mechanisms. *American Journal of Orthopsychiatry* 57:316–31.

2. Meyers, J., & Wilcox, B. (1998). Public policy applications of research on violence and children. In Trickett & Schellenbach (Eds.), *Violence against children in the family and in the community* (pp. 465–78). Washington, DC: American Psychological Association.

3. New Freedom Commission on Mental Health. (2003). *Achieving the promise: Transforming mental health care in America. Final Report.* DHHS Pub. No. SMA-03-3832. Rockville, MD.

INDEX

211

ABOUT THE AUTHOR

Daniel J. Flannery resides in Cleveland, Ohio, with his wife Caroline and their four children. He is currently Professor of Justice Studies and director of the Institute for the Study and Prevention of Violence at Kent State University. He is also a licensed clinical psychologist and an Associate Professor of Pediatrics at Case Western Reserve University and University Hospitals of Cleveland. He was coeditor (with C. R. Huff) of *Youth Violence: Prevention, Intervention and Social Policy* (1999) for American Psychiatric Press. His primary areas of interest are in youth violence prevention, the link between violence and mental health, and program evaluation. He received his PhD in 1991 in clinical child psychology from The Ohio State University. His previous appointments were as Assistant Professor of Family Studies at the University of Arizona and Associate Professor of child psychiatry at Case Western Reserve University. He has served as consultant to various local and national organizations including the U.S. departments of Justice and Education, the Centers for Disease Control and Prevention, the National Crime Prevention Council, and the National Resource Center for Safe Schools.